FIRE PLACES

FIRE PLACES

A Practical Design Guide to Fireplaces and Stoves Indoors and Out

JANE GITLIN

The Taunton Press

The Taunton Press, Inc., 63 South Main Street, PO Box 5506, Newtown, CT 06470-5506
e-mail: tp@taunton.com

Editors: Erica Sanders-Foege and Jennifer Renjilian Morris
Jacket/Cover design: Chris Thompson
Interior design: Renato Stanisic
Layout: Renato Stanisic
Illustrator: Vincent Babak

Library of Congress Cataloging-in-Publication Data

Gitlin, Jane.
Fire places : a practical design guide to fireplaces and stoves indoors and out / Jane Gitlin.
p. cm.
ISBN-13: 978-1-56158-835-0
ISBN-10: 1-56158-835-0
1. Fireplaces--Design and construction. 2. Stoves, Wood--Design and construction. I. Title.
TH7425.G58 2006
697'.1--dc22
2006011273

Printed in Singapore
10 9 8 7 6 5 4 3

The following manufacturers/names appearing in *Fire Places* are trademarks:
Boeing®, Heat & Glo®, Sterno®, UL®, Yellow Pages®

For those in my heart and at my hearthside: Mack, David, and Michael

Acknowledgments

Over the last several months I have spoken and corresponded with many helpful and knowledgeable people. I wish I could meet each of these individuals to thank them personally for pointing me in the right direction, answering my queries, graciously contributing knowledge, sharing expertise, and expediting images, but a virtual hearty handshake will have to suffice: Richard "Jiggs" Blackburn, Jim Buckley, Susanna M. Crampton, Gordon Flagler, Melissa Jay, Ola Lessard, Sara the Stove Princess, Edward Semmelroth, and Richard S. Young.

The following manufacturers generously furnished photos, and I thank them and their cordial and helpful staff members for their contributions: American Energy Systems Inc., American Gas Log Company Inc., Burley Appliances Ltd., CFM Products, the Chimney Pot Shoppe, Condar Company, Dell-Point Pellet Stoves, Fire Rock Mfg. Inc., Fireorb/Cool Warmth Company, Heat & Glo, Lennox Hearth Products, Moberg Fireplaces, Solus Décor Inc., Sud-Chemie Prototech Inc., and Trikeenan Tileworks, Inc.

A project of this scope cannot be completed without lots of help, and I gratefully acknowledge my colleagues, friends, and family for fanning the creative flames with their hospitality, perspective, meals, books, technical assistance, and the most valuable gifts of time and friendship; in particular: Eric and Lori Braun, Colin and Ellen Cool, Deirdre Fahy, Michael Ferguson, Friends of Middlebrook, Tanya Gillette, David Gorbach, Kevin Huelster, Susan Lawrence, Audrey Locorotondo, Amy Mezoff, Caroline Labiner Moser, Lynne Porter, John Runia, Samuel Wurzel, and Uri Yokel.

A picture is worth a thousand words, and the gorgeous images of many gifted photographers, skilled graphic designers, and talented illustrators do better in pictures than I can even put into words, and I thank each of them for their contributions.

My sincere thanks to the creative and editorial staff at Taunton Press: Peter Chapman, Jim Childs, Steve Culpepper, Julie Hamilton, Carolyn Mandarano, Wendi Mijal, Jennifer Peters, Seth Reichgott, Jennifer Renjilian Morris, and Erica Sanders-Foege, for their professionalism and patience and for entrusting me with this project. It was a slow race to completion, and I welcome Henry, who beat me to the finish line.

And finally, my love and thanks to the fellows who share my hearth and warm my heart: David, Mack, and Michael Nishball.

Contents

CHAPTER 4

CHAPTER 5

CHAPTER 6

Introduction

What more appealing scene can you conjure up on a wintry day than a pair of comfortable armchairs pulled up to a crackling fire while wisps of smoke curl from the chimney top? All your senses are in use—the sight of the flickering flames, the sound of the crackling logs, the warmth on your face, and the fragrance and taste of wood smoke. Certainly this image is a cliché; nevertheless, the hearth truly is the essential core of every home, whether it is an actual fireplace, a sturdy stove, or merely a mantel shelf displaying the treasures and trophies of intertwined lives. No longer used solely for practical uses like cooking or heating, a fireplace is the fundamental symbol of Home: the domestic core of warmth and nourishment.

Those of us lucky to have one or more fire places in our homes treat them with a particular reverence. We adorn the mantelpieces with our prized possessions, we pose for formal photos in front of them, and we decorate them each season in almost a shrinelike manner. Buying or selling a house is sure to underscore the value of a fire place on the list of the home's top amenities, and adding a new fire place to our existing homes indicates our commitment to the place by imprinting our enduring mark.

But fireplaces are more than a mere brick hole in the wall for burning logs, and stoves are more than a fire in a cast iron box. They include a host of other parts and pieces and accessories to keep them burning attractively and safely. There are the architectural parts—the sturdy chimneys, hearths and fireboxes that make up the shape of the fireplace or stove. There are the decorative parts–the gorgeous mantelpieces, handmade tile or honed granite surrounds, dramatic chimneys and quirky chimney pots–that give style and substance. And there are parts that we can't even see–the dampers, flues, and ash pits–that keep our fires blazing safely. The traditional hand-built masonry fireplace and chimney is only one way to attain a hearth within your home. These days, you are just as apt to encounter a wood-burning stove, gas-fired flames, or an array of candles in place of a stack of logs.

There is a fireplace or a stove for every budget, too, from a prefabricated unit to a craftsman-built monument. A visit to a specialty home shop will introduce you to the wide variety of outdoor fireplaces and fire pits now available for toasting marshmallows on a crisp evening. And no fireplace or stove is complete without a few accessories and tools that personalize it and keep the flames alight, such as screens, andirons, firedogs, grates, pokers, bellows, and brooms. Whether you are planning a new fireplace for your home, recasting an existing one, or shopping for a stove, there are a lot of choices of materials and finishes available to you. What are the best selections? That will depend on the building codes, your budget, and your personal style. The hundreds of photographs in this book will reveal the range of options for all flavors and varieties while outlining the parameters for the design–all the fancy features and the necessary components that will keep your home fire burning. I invite you to pull up your armchair to the hearth, and take a look through this gallery of ideas for your own home.

"A fire place brings the ambience and beauty of a hearth into your home."

CHAPTER

1

Your Fire Place

FIRE IS MAGICAL AND DANGEROUS AND USEFUL, ALL AT THE SAME TIME. SINCE THE BEGINNING OF HUMAN HISTORY, FIRE HAS PLAYED A CRUCIAL ROLE IN OUR LIVES, AND ALTHOUGH IT IS NO LONGER NECESSARY TO OUR SURVIVAL, FIRE STILL LURES US WITH ITS BEAUTY AND COMFORT. YOU'D BE HARD-PRESSED TO FIND SOMEONE WHO DOESN'T WANT A FIREPLACE SOMEWHERE IN THEIR HOME. TODAY'S FIRESIDE IS NOT LIMITED TO A CAMPFIRE IN A CLEARING OR EVEN YOUR GRANDMOTHER'S BRICK HEARTH. ALONG WITH THE TRADITIONAL, WOOD-BURNING MASONRY FIREPLACE, YOU CAN FIND A PREFABRICATED metal or insert fireplace that burns wood or gas, or a cast iron stove in any shape or size. You can have a stand-alone fireplace, a masonry heater, a fire pit, or a newfangled fire display. You can even find electric "fireplaces" that mimic the look of flickering flames and can be installed just about anywhere.

Fire places are cropping up in unexpected places, like bathrooms and kitchens, and alongside patios and porches. And they are increasingly popular in unexpected regions of the United States, like the air-conditioned homes of Florida and Hawaii. Whether your front yard features a snowbank, a grapefruit tree, or city traffic, a fire place brings the ambience and beauty of a hearth into your home.

FACING PAGE: Even with modern lighting, heating, and cooking appliances, we still desire the warmth and beauty of a fireplace in our homes.

LEFT: A hearth acts as the focus of a room. Artfully crafted stonework gives the hearth beauty and personality.

RITUAL AND CULTURE

The mystery of fire's origins has captivated us since human history began. Early civilizations explained fire as a gift to us from the gods, a surprise that falls out of the sky, or a substance that smolders below the ground in a spirit realm. In every known human culture, fire has had a sacred nature, honored in story and ceremony.

Fire Mythology

Here are some representatives from the pantheon of gods and goddesses of fire and the rites that honored them:

- **Loki, the Scandinavian fire demon, is a legendary mischief maker, and today when flames are crackling in Norwegian hearths they say that Loki is thrashing his children.**
- **Agni, the fire god of the ancient Persians, is a red man with three legs and seven arms who rides a ram while fire spews from his mouth. He is born by rubbing together two pieces of wood, and when he emerges as a flame he devours his parents. He dwells in every hearth and protects the home.**
- **The early peoples of South America revered the fire god Xiuhtecuhtli. To honor him, at the end of every 52-year cycle all fires were extinguished and a fresh one was kindled on a prisoner's breast in order to keep time moving.**
- **Pagan Slavs worshipped fire itself—Svarogich, born of the sky. Even today there is respect shown in Slavic homes when the fire is being kindled, and children are cautioned not to shout or swear.**
- **Ancient Japanese had to placate the fire god Ho-Masubi, the causer of fire, to protect their wooden homes from destruction.**
- **Polynesians revered Maui, who stole fire for them from the keeper of the underworld.**
- **The Bushmen of southern Africa light large fires to create dark clouds of smoke to entice the rain to fall.**
- **Ukko, the supreme god of the pagan Finns, created fire by striking his fingernail against his sword, creating a spark that traveled through the air into a lake where it was snapped up by a succession of fish and finally freed by the hero Väinämöinen.**
- **Roman mythology includes Vesta, the goddess of fire, who looked after the domestic hearth. Vestal virgins were Roman girls selected from patrician families who entered Vesta's service for 30 years and presided over ceremonies involving a sacred fire and pure water.**

Probably the most familiar tale is that of Prometheus. In the Greek myth, Zeus, the supreme deity, withheld fire from mankind because he was angry about a trick that Prometheus, a mere mortal, had played on him. Prometheus retaliated by stealing a firebrand from the forges of Hephaestus and transporting this flame in a hollow stalk, thus returning the gift of fire to man. Today, in the weeks leading up to the Olympic Games, runners replay this scene when they relay to the site of the modern games a torch lit at the ruins of the Temple of Hera.

Ancient lore and ritual have followed fire into modern times and our homes today. When we decorate our fireplace mantels to honor a holiday season or light candles to practice a religious rite, we acknowledge the role of fire in our ethnic traditions, our religious backgrounds, and our heritage. Even secular events and holidays are often celebrated with a bonfire.

FACING PAGE: Firelight and candles create an ambience that cannot be duplicated by artificial lighting. The fire captures our glances and soothes our thoughts.

LEFT: The leaves strewn across the frieze of the mantelpiece spring from the jambs that are on either side of the fireplace's opening. Trees and leaves are an appropriate decoration that underscore the organic origins of fire.

Ancient ritual or cultural tradition? Hanging stockings at the fireplace for Santa Claus is not so different than expecting favors from a fire god as reward for good behavior.

Fireside Lore

SANTA CLAUS

The character of Santa Claus has its origins in the pagan god Thor, who was represented as a genial and tubby old man with a long white beard. He rode in a chariot pulled by two goats named Gnasher and Cracker. His element was fire and his color red. He was a protector god who looked after and helped humans. The fireplace was his sacred place, and he would enter homes through chimneys and thus into the fire.

TAMING FIRE

We can only imagine how early humans realized that the fire ignited by a lightning bolt in a storm could be cultivated to burn, heat, and cook. Some enterprising soul in each early community must have discovered that rubbing two sticks together made enough friction to light dried moss for tinder, which could then be used to ignite larger pieces of dried wood for a full-fledged fire. Much later came the monumental discovery that fire could be created by striking flint onto iron pyrite, and, still later, onto steel.

For thousands of years, fire-starting kits containing fire steels, bags of flammable tinder, and flint stones were common personal items. By the mid 19th century, quick-flaming matches were being manufactured in England and in the Americas. Today, the battery-operated fire starter eliminates even the need to strike a match, and the art of striking a fire with flint has petered out.

In general, household technology has accelerated over the last hundred years at an incredible pace. In a few short generations we've abandoned cast iron cookers for self-cleaning ovens and exchanged our oil lanterns for halogen lights. We no longer need an open fire or a cast iron stove to heat our rooms, to cook our meals, or to ward off the dark. A fireplace is as practical today as a buggy whip. Nevertheless, old and new houses have them. Is it habit, nostalgia, superstition, or the persistent idea of the hearth as the core of the home?

KEEPING THE HOME FIRES BURNING

Once we had tamed it, humans became reliant upon fire. Early societies faced the challenge to create a fire when and where they needed it, preserve a fire while they were using it, and stop a fire before it became a hazard. In terms of both construction and design, most fireplaces and many of the stoves available in North America today have roots in colonial times.

ABOVE: Fireplace accessories and the items we place near the fire are often practical safety devices, but they can also express a homeowner's passions, like a love of the sea or a memorable vacation.

LEFT: Better than any banner, a roaring fire and a couple of comfy chairs is as obvious a welcome home sign as there is. A fireplace at the center of the house will radiate heat in all directions within the house, and there is a cost savings by not having a large, exposed chimney outdoors.

Fireside Lore

CHUCK MUCKS

The Chinese created the first all-in-one lighters, called "chuck mucks," which were fabric pouches to hold tinder with the flint and steel sewn in. Some early Scandinavians fashioned polished crystals that could aim a beam of sunlight on tinder and ignite a fire by the power of the sun.

A niche in the stonework is the perfect spot to showcase a favorite painting, and the mantel shelf is an obvious spot to place candles and family photos.

Fireside Lore

MATCHES

The invention of the safety match was based on the 1680 English discovery that phosphorus and sulfur would burst into flame if rubbed together. In 1836, American Alonzo Phillips obtained a patent for wooden "friction matches" that he dubbed "Locofocos." In 1889, an American lawyer named Joshua Pusey invented paper book matches and sold his patent to the Diamond Match Company, which still produces them today.

Colonial fireplaces

At the beginning of the 17th century, all but the crudest of dwellings constructed by European settlers had a working fireplace of some type. The New World pioneers brought time-honored methods for building fireplaces based on the materials they had readily available in Europe and the particular, traditional ways they interacted with their fireplaces in their homelands.

The English favored a large fireplace to heat each principal room of a dwelling and to provide a source of heat for indoor cooking. Dutch, German, and Scandinavian settlers brought the cast iron stove, which would morph, with the help of inventor Benjamin Franklin, into the efficient Franklin stove that warmed many North American homes for decades.

Like every other technology in history, fireplace construction in North America moved ahead by trial and error. The "catted chimneys" of timber and clay used by English colonists proved a poor choice for their thatched-roof homes. By the mid 17th century, brick was the preferred material for fireplaces and chimneys throughout the colonies.

The bricks were originally laid in place with mortar made from clay, a locally abundant substance. But clay could not withstand the harsh elements. Instead, weather-resistant lime was imported for many years until limestone beds were discovered in the colonies. For a time, burnt oyster shells were used as a passable substitute for lime mortar, although chimneys made with them were also vulnerable to cold, damp weather.

Fireside Lore

CURFEW

In the 11th century a metal cover called a "curfew" was developed to extinguish flames and cover the hot embers until morning. Bells would ring to signal that it was time to cover the communal fire with the curfew. We still invoke a curfew at times to curtail the evening's activities and send everyone scurrying home.

A central chimneystack that could accommodate more than one fireplace was the literal core of Colonial-era homes. This newer home carries on the tradition.

6¢

FACING PAGE: Today this is a quaint scene, but in the 17th century this was the center of family life. The fire burned year-round for cooking, and needed constant tending.

LEFT: Brick has historically been the material of choice for crafting the hearth. You can build walls and floors, and even a perfect Roman arch, with one basic fireproof module.

The configuration and location of fireplaces varied from region to region. In the South, fireplaces were used primarily for cooking. They were located at the ends of a building or even in a kitchen outbuilding to prevent the house from overheating and as a precaution against fires. Cooking and heating water for laundry were all-day chores, so the fire burned long hours. In the Northeast, a working fireplace was the difference between surviving and freezing to death during cruel winters. Fireplaces were clustered at the center of the house, so that the single large brick chimneystack could radiate heat into the surrounding rooms.

Considering the amount of space the fireplace occupied in a room, the colonial fireplace-and-chimney construction (known collectively as a chimneystack) heated a room inefficiently. The fire would certainly burn hot—evidenced by the singe marks on a typical fireplace's massive wooden lintel—but most of the heat was expelled up the chimney instead of into the room. Shivering colonists found their front sides were toasty while their backsides stayed frosty. Wing-backed chairs and high-backed benches called settles were designed to ward off drafts and allow one to soak in the heat at the hearth.

RIGHT: Modern innovations in stove technology provide fuel-efficient and attractive alternatives to a fireplace. The view of the flames remains intact, as does the scent of wood smoke.

Improvements and innovations

It took two 18th-century Benjamins, Mr. Thompson and Mr. Franklin, to independently study the problem of smoky, inefficient fireplaces and to design two remarkable alternatives. Benjamin Thompson, known as Count Rumford, devised new geometries to design masonry fireplaces with shallower and taller fireboxes that permitted more heat to radiate outward into a room. The Franklin stove was a freestanding cast iron firebox that reduced the amount of smoke from a household fire and released clean, warmed air into the room. The Franklin stove, or "Pennsylvania Fireplace," borrowed its basic concept from the plate stoves introduced to North America by Dutch, Scandinavian, and German settlers.

The Art of Fire

Colonial Cooking

Cooking was done in iron pots hung on hooks that swiveled over the flames. Hall or keeping room (kitchen) fireplaces incorporated bake ovens as well. Early bake ovens were built to the rear of the firebox, a hazard to women in long skirts who had to dodge the flames to bake their bread. Later, the brick "beehive" oven was built to the side of the fireplace. A beehive oven has a firebox below and a baking chamber with a cast iron door on top. The fire was started early in the day to heat the oven space above. An experienced baker could stick her arm into the oven and gauge if the temperature was hot enough to bake her daily bread. Once the temperature was hot enough, the fire below was extinguished or allowed to burn out, and the day's baking would commence.

The plate stove's primary function was cooking, but it nicely heated the room in which it stood. The earliest models were formed of interlocking cast iron plates, often decoratively molded with biblical scenes or proverbs. Local cast iron foundries sprang up across the colonies to manufacture the plates, as well as kettles and other household utensils.

The early five-plate stove had a firebox left open to an adjacent brick or stone fireplace to share its chimney for venting. The next-generation plate stove was called a close stove or Holland stove. It sat away from the wall and independent of the fireplace, with a closed, cast iron back that could be opened to feed the fire. A separate flue connected the Holland stove's firebox to the fireplace's chimney nearby.

Before the American Revolution, English colonists further improved efficiency with the ten-plate stove, which had a separate chamber for baking. This stove, the precursor to 19th-century cook stoves, replaced the masonry bake ovens that were built alongside older fireplaces or outdoors in bake houses. Stoves and fireplaces continued to go their separate ways.

By the turn of the 20th century, the distinction between a utility stove for cooking and a fireplace for socializing was well established. Rather than become obsolete, the fireplace was transformed into a fresh canvas for the architect and the homemaker. The eternal human desire for a hearth had found a new outlet, and the concept of the visually pleasing home fireplace was making inroads in North American architecture and life.

ABOVE: This tile-bedecked fireplace needs no applied mantelpiece to draw your eye. Handmade tiles cover the entire surface, capturing the heat and radiating it over several hours.

LEFT: From plate-stove components cast in sand to modern versions of a stove made from spun steel, metal vessels for holding fire can be fabricated and marketed, unlike hand-built fireplaces.

warmed, but a person sitting to the side of the fireplace or far away from it will not. Someone in an adjacent room may feel the warmth generated by a stove, but will be left out in the cold by a lit fireplace crackling elsewhere in the house.

Stoves nicely heat a small, confined space and can provide enough heat to circulate into several rooms. For an outdoor site, such as a patio, a fireplace may be a better choice for drawing a crowd on a cold night; it will heat the people who gather around it and not squander its warmth in the outside air.

Lack of a backyard woodlot shouldn't prevent you from enjoying a fire. In the same way that we don't have to hunt to eat, we don't have to fell our own trees to obtain logs to burn. Fuel is easier than ever to procure. Even if you live in a New York City skyscraper you can order bundles of firewood for delivery right to your door or purchase a manufactured log at the supermarket for 90 minutes of flickering flames. Natural gas is piped into many homes, and gas-fueled fireplaces or stoves can be ignited with a push of a button. Biomass fuels like pellets or corn are by-products of the timber and farming industry and can be purchased by the bagful. Electric fireplaces can be mounted in any location near a power outlet.

ABOVE: The double-height spaces that appear so often in contemporary homes require a strong architectural statement, which a fireplace and tall chimney can provide.

RIGHT: The taller-than-wider proportions of this fireplace's opening extend to the mantelpiece, almost dwarfing the furnishings and making a dramatic arrangement.

FACING PAGE: A beautiful fire screen can be a substitute for a television or computer screen, and even when there is no fire burning the fire-place remains a captivating centerpiece.

WHAT'S YOUR FIRE PLACE?

Like the phoenix rising from its own ashes, the age-old fire place has emerged as a significant and desirable architectural feature, unrelated to cooking or heating. To choose the right fire place, you need to know why you want a one.

Heat

If you are seeking a heating source, consider whether you plan to heat one room or several and whether the fireplace will be the sole source of heat for a space.

A stove can heat a room better than a fireplace because it is designed to heat the air. An open fireplace is a radiant heater; it heats only what it can "see." A person directly facing the fireplace will be

FACING PAGE: Rustic homes demand rustic fireplaces. The stone of this fireplace matches the home's stone foundation, tying together the building materials and forms.

LEFT: Stoves are easier to add to an existing room because they are not as heavy as a masonry fireplace. They are also great supplemental heat sources.

BOTTOM: Gas fireplaces have become very popular in bedrooms because of their easy on/easy off control switches. They are also cleaner because they don't require logs or need their ashes emptied.

Mood

If ambience is your primary goal, the sky's the limit. First, consider the best placement in your home for a fire place. Where do you want people to gather? Which room deserves, or needs, the drama of a fire place? Once these decisions are made, you can choose a fire place that is physically, technically, and visually suitable for the space you have in mind.

Cooking

Do you want to cook in your fire place? Most indoor fire places are impractical for cooking, although many a bowl of old-fashioned popcorn has been popped in the traditional fireplace, and some stovetops do get hot enough to brew a pot of tea. If you want more cooking function, you'll really have to design for it with a custom-built bread/pizza oven or barbeque, or purchase some of the newer fangled fireplace cooking implements on the market.

A HEARTH FOR EVERY ROOM

There is no single, correct location for a fireplace or stove. Much depends on your home's décor and how you use your rooms. Traditionally, in colder

RIGHT: Having a wood-burning oven in your kitchen means you can authentically bake bread or pizza right at home.

BELOW: Even the smallest fireplace can look grand and inviting when surrounded by a substantial stone surround and chunky mantel shelf.

Fireside Lore

A LITERARY CHIMNEY

"Within thirty feet of the turf-sided road, my chimney—a huge, corpulent old Harry VIII of a chimney—rises full in front of me and all my possessions. Standing well up a hillside, my chimney, like Lord Rosse's monster telescope, swung vertical to hit the meridian moon, is the first object to greet the approaching traveler's eye, nor is it the last which the sun salutes. My chimney, too, is before me in receiving the first-fruits of the seasons. The snow is on its head ere on my hat; and every spring, as in a hollow beech tree, the first swallows build their nests in it."

—HERMAN MELVILLE, "I AND MY CHIMNEY"

climates, fireplaces were located smack in the middle of a principal room of a home. In warmer climates, where the need for heat was less intense, a fireplace was often placed against a wall. Today, a room's function, size, proportion, and configuration in the floor plan of the house need to be evaluated, as well as the style and arrangement of furnishings for that room.

We typically see fireplaces in living rooms and family rooms, where they provide a unique focal point and anchor the room architecturally. We spend a lot of time in those rooms entertaining and relaxing, so we strive to create just the right domestic ambience as a backdrop for our families and ourselves. In an often-seen or much-used room, the fireplace mantelpiece is the prime spot for display of our most cherished possessions and favorite pieces of art. If you look through your own family photo album, no doubt there are plenty of shots of your family and friends all dressed up, posing with the fireplace as the backdrop.

ABOVE: A simple mantel shelf can still have impact. The space acts as a miniature gallery for photos and artwork.

LEFT: Raising the level of the hearth to counter height in this kitchen puts it at eye level for everyone seated at the table, and the firelight enhances the mood at every meal.

Fireplaces and stoves are seen more often today in the rooms where we gather for meals. Eating alongside a cheery fire hearkens back to the day when all our food was cooked over an open flame. A fireplace in the dining room complements lit candles on the table and encourages us to linger over brandy or coffee. When a dining room table dominates the furnishings, especially in a small room, the fireplace adds cachet without taking up floor space.

Before the advent of the cook stove, kitchens always had fireplaces, and the fire burned almost continuously to prepare meals and bake bread. Today you can find fireplaces and stoves designed into modern kitchens for decoration and for cooking, with indoor barbecues or bread/pizza ovens.

What better way to spend a quiet evening at home than curled up with a book stove-side or with a sweetheart in front of a romantic fire? More and more frequently we find fireplaces and stoves

ABOVE: A mantelpiece can go beyond just a frame for the fireplace. This custom-designed mantel incorporates unusual materials to create a graphic composition that enhances the décor.

RIGHT: Pairing a fireplace with a hot tub is popular in vacation homes or anywhere you want the luxury of toweling off before the fire. Using gas to fuel the fire means you can start a fire whenever you get the urge to hit the tub and not worry about taking the time to build a wood fire.

showing up in nontraditional corners of the home, such as dens, libraries, master bedrooms, and even fancy bathrooms. New, prefabricated fireplace inserts, smaller stoves, and alternative fuels provide affordable options that are easy to install and appropriate for spaces not initially designed to hold a full-scale fireplace. There is also room for whimsy in a petite fireplace. Gas and electric fireplaces and stoves even have remote control switches that offer such luxuries as turning on the fire as you step into the bathtub and extinguishing it with the touch of a button at bedtime.

Fireplaces are not just for indoor rooms, though. As more and more homeowners create outdoor rooms, fire places are moving back outside. You can purchase an assortment of prefabricated devices, such as metal fire pits and ceramic chimineas, that draw friends and family together on a cool night. Or consider a site-built fireplace that stands alone in the landscape or is incorporated into the configuration of the house; these can range from very simple to the architecturally elaborate.

Basking in the light and warmth of any type of fireplace, indoors or out, is a delightful sensation. The living fire awakens our primitive instincts and connects us to our prehistoric ancestors who depended on fire for their essential needs and gathered around it for companionship.

ABOVE: This fireplace extends a stone arm that invites you to sit and stay a while.

LEFT: An outdoor fireplace lets you use your terrace or veranda late into the evening or late into the season, providing a region of comforting heat and fire glow against the nighttime or cold.

“Including a fireplace in our home is rarely a necessity, but most of us would like to have one.”

CHAPTER

2

Fireplaces

WE LOVE OUR FIREPLACES. LOGS CRACKLING, A HINT OF WOODSMOKE IN THE AIR. FEW CAN DENY THE APPEAL OF SITTING BY THE HEARTH AND EXPERIENCING SUCH WARMTH. DESPITE THE FACT THAT MOST OF OUR HOMES TODAY ARE HEATED BY SOME COMBINATION OF FURNACE AND FORCED AIR OR BOILER AND BASEBOARD HEAT, WE STILL CRAVE A FIREPLACE. IT'S LIKE INSISTING ON AN ANALOG CLOCK IN A DIGITAL DEVICE PURELY FOR THE SIGHT OF A FAMILIAR FACE. THERE IS SIMPLY NO ROMANCE IN CURLING UP ALONGSIDE A RADIATOR, SO IT'S NO SURPRISE THAT MORE AND MORE PEOPLE WHOSE HOMES LACK A FIREPLACE ARE taking the time and money to either add one or renovate an existing one. This is a serious undertaking and there are many things to consider.

If you have little working knowledge of fireplaces, it's important to understand the basic distinctions between types of fireplaces, the fuel they burn, and their aesthetic style. The primary distinction is between the hand-built masonry type of fireplace, which is constructed on site by a skilled mason, and prefabricated metal fireplaces—called appliances or zero-clearance fireplaces—that are selected from a showroom or catalog and installed by a contractor.

Both sorts of fireplaces—masonry and prefabricated—are set up to burn either wood or gas and can run the gamut from massive site-built structures erected brick by brick to manufactured models that can be installed in a day. Understanding the differences between the types is important in determining what type is right for your purposes and evaluating your selection.

FACING PAGE: The fireplace is part of the architecture of a room rather than merely a decoration. Including an exposed chimney in a two-story room draws the eye upward to the roof trusses.

LEFT: Traditional wood-burning masonry-type fireplaces are found in thousands of homes. They range from simple brick structures to massive stone designs.

RIGHT: The pairing of fireplace and bench creates a room within a room. Creating these sorts of nooks in your home will encourage you to light a fire and use your fireplace more often.

FACING PAGE: The fireplace is just one ingredient in a paneled wall that combines shelving, seating, display space, and the hearth. This combination is a formula for comfort.

WHAT SORT OF FIREPLACE FOR YOUR HOME?

Of course, the type of fireplace you select is influenced by its configuration and orientation to the room. Your fireplace may sit along a wall, appear in a corner, or be prominently located in the middle of a large room. If you're renovating, you may not have the luxury of placing your fireplace just where you'd like it, but if you are building from scratch you have the chance to locate your new fireplace to best suit your preferences, your home's style and character, and, naturally, your budget.

Style

Most fireplace types can be fashioned into a particular style that flatters your house, whether it is a stone mansion or a modest bungalow. By style, I mean the way it looks—its more decorative aspects and how it can accentuate the architectural and interior design of your home. For example, the fireplace style that goes best with a Georgian style colonial has neoclassical details on a white mantelpiece. A two-story family room in a western lodge is all the more dramatic when a stone chimney rises up through the space, allowing your eye to track up to the rafters. A farmhouse living room, on the other hand, is made even cozier by a fireplace with built-in benches and storage alongside the hearth.

Your fireplace is the signature of the room that it embellishes, so it needs to fit its environment. Personal preferences and pet peeves will surely influence any stylistic choices you make, but a little knowledge of architectural history and regional varieties will help you. Later in this chapter I've outlined some of the major architectural styles, but your own personal style, whether it leans toward contemporary or antique, can still be adapted for your home.

ABOVE: The brick is left exposed, revealing the soldier course, a line of upright bricks that forms the lintel above the firebox. Using high-quality finish bricks on the interior saves the cost of applying any other finishes.

FACING PAGE: A fireplace doesn't need to be an elaborate or expensive proposition to be successful. If the fire draws well, the company is congenial, and the conversation is flowing, then the fireplace is a success.

Budget

Custom-built fireplaces are expensive. You can expect to pay $10,000 or more for one with a lot of bells and whistles, such as multiple faces, an unusual chimney, and costly materials. It is possible, though, to build a simple brick fireplace for around $2,000.

A manufactured fireplace offers an alternative to a custom-built one and, depending on its features, can be less expensive. The general perception is that prefabricated fireplaces are less expensive than site-built ones because they are manufactured, as opposed to built on site, so the cost of labor is not passed on to the customer. The truth is that prefabricated fireplaces can cost more than site-built masonry ones, depending on the installation. A prefab's special features and accessories, like motorized blowers, expensive tile surround, or custom glass doors, will increase the expense and can end up costing more than a basic site-built brick fireplace.

To evaluate the precise differences, you'll need to compare the costs of each component of the fireplace, including the chimney. A fireplace is a

complex system of parts and should be assembled by an experienced mason, contractor, or installer, so be sure to factor that cost into your budget. And don't forget the cost of yearly maintenance, which is required to keep your fireplace working efficiently and safely.

MASONRY FIREPLACES

An open-faced wood-burning masonry fireplace is most likely found in a house built before the invention of central heating. You'll also find the same masonry fireplace in homes built recently, but in spite of its shortcomings—the expense of building it, its relative inefficiency in delivering any real heat compared to central heating, and its annual maintenance—the traditional fireplace is still popular.

Masonry fireplaces in older homes are primarily designed to burn wood, and newer versions follow this model. Wood is a common, easily obtained fuel; it takes no special fittings or hookups and is widely available at a reasonable price. Nothing comes close to duplicating wood's particular fragrance and

ABOVE: The monumental stone surround not only adds visual heft to this fireplace, but also stores heat radiated from the flames and is agreeably warm to the touch.

RIGHT: Glass fireplace doors keep warmed room air from being carried up the chimney, but they do cut down on the amount of radiant heat from the fire that reaches people and objects in the room.

character as it burns, although gas and even electric fireplaces offer a pretty good approximation.

Masonry, the all-purpose word referring to the stone, brick, or concrete materials that form the bulk of the fireplace, is a fireproof container for the burning fuel and a channel for hot gas and smoke. The solid masonry also absorbs the warmth from the flames and releases it slowly over a series of hours, which makes it a heat source long after the fire has burned out.

Improving efficiency

The classic masonry fireplace with its deep, open firebox has been found to be anywhere from 10 percent to 55 percent efficient, but the results depend a great deal on the testing methods and the individual fireplace. In a fireplace, the fire emits radiant energy that heats nearby objects, not the air, so conventional efficiency test methods don't measure the actual sensation of warmth you get when sitting by the fire. It's like sitting under the bright sun on a cool day—the air around you is cool, but you feel warm. Much of the heated air is lost up the chimney instead of directed back into the room. When no fire is burning, there may also be passive heat loss through the fireplace, especially if the damper has been left open.

There is a newer generation of more efficient masonry fireplaces, called air-circulating fireplaces, that are better at delivering heated air into the room. They have vents located under the firebox that draw in fresh room air, circulate it around the firebox, and then release the heated air through vents in the upper portion of the fireplace, sometimes aided by a gentle blower. This improves the distribution of warmed air and the efficiency of the fireplace to a degree, but it isn't always possible to retrofit an older fireplace with this feature. Building codes now require a fresh-air supply vent for new fireplaces, but for preexisting fireplaces cracking a window or door might be the only solution to bring in fresh air to keep the fire from smoldering.

There are several things you can do so that your wood-burning masonry fireplace burns properly, safely, cleanly, and at its maximum efficiency. First, make sure that the damper is fully opened. Second, burn only dry, well-seasoned wood. Third, regularly maintain and clean your chimney. Accumulation of creosote (a flammable compound) or animal and bird's-nest debris can restrict airflow. Finally, make sure there is enough air in the room for combustion, or the fire will burn feebly, causing a smokier burn and providing less heat.

On Fire

Efficiency Ratings

A fuel-burning device's efficiency is the percentage of the total energy content of a given fuel (wood, gas, or biomass) that is transferred into the air in the house instead of up the chimney. Methods of measuring efficiency vary, and because open fireplaces warm objects and people directly through radiation and closed stoves warm the air through convection, it is difficult to compare them. You may find it toasty enough sitting near an open fire even if the room's air temperature measures lower than it might if you were using a stove instead. An optimal efficiency for either a fireplace or stove would be 70 percent to 80 percent efficient.

Building a Masonry Fireplace

If you could build a masonry fireplace after a trip to the home center and complete it over the weekend, there'd be a fireplace in every room in the house. In reality, the challenge of a masonry fireplace is a task

The Art of Fire

Masons

All fireplace builders are masons, but not all masons have the experience to build a fireplace. It is a craft that takes skill and years of experience to master.

When considering hiring a mason, look for membership in one of the respected trade organizations (see Resources, p. 194) or certification as a Certified Brick Mason or Certified Rumford Mason. Of course, the best recommendation a craftsman can have is that of a satisfied customer. Ask for references and a portfolio to review.

BOTTOM: This fireplace is ready for its inset hearthstone, stone cladding, and mantel to be installed. The fresh-air intake at the front helps to diminish the amount of warm room air needed to keep the fire ablaze.

FACING PAGE: Stones come in many hues. Selecting your fireplace's color palette is just as important as selecting the shape and coursing of your stonework to compliment the decor and architecture.

best left to the experts. There are calculations and building code requirements to follow, not to mention the skill in handling concrete, block, brick, and stone. In addition, the fireplace itself is only the visible portion of a larger construction that includes a foundation and chimney.

THE FOUNDATION — A masonry fireplace is a massive structure that can weigh several tons and requires a solid foundation to bear the weight of the stone, brick, and concrete block. The ground must be excavated to just below the frost line to ensure a solid base for the foundation; otherwise, the foundation may shift. If the foundation shifts because it is too small or not deep enough in the ground to withstand frost heave, the rest of the chimneystack will also shift and cracks will form. This is dangerous because cracks loosen bricks, and these openings can allow the poisonous carbon monoxide that is in the gas emitted by a fire to make its way into the house.

The size of the foundation is determined by the building code and is, at minimum, 12 in. thick at the bottom of the entire fireplace structure including the chimney, and extends out 6 in. beyond its exterior dimensions. The foundation may also include a concrete extension under the floor level to support a hearthstone or brick hearth. This foundation is usually poured at the same time as the foundation for the house, because negotiating a concrete pour into an existing basement or crawl space is much trickier. However, adding a new foundation for a fireplace at the perimeter of an existing house can be done fairly easily and is not too disruptive to the existing structure or its inhabitants.

THE FIREBOX AND HEARTH — There are strict building code regulations that govern the dimensions, proportions, and overall construction of a fireplace. In simplest terms, the basic shape of

Minding the Codes

The International Residential Code (IRC) is the national legal building regulations that homes and fireplaces must follow. Individual states may enact stricter regulations or modify those outlined in the code. The purpose of the IRC is to ensure life safety by legislating safe construction methods and standards. Chapter 10 of the 2003 IRC deals with residential fireplaces and chimneys and sets forth minimum clearances between the fireplace and the nearest combustible materials, like the wooden mantelpiece or the surrounding wood framing or flooring. The size of the hearth extension is based on the area of the fireplace opening, and the width of the surround is a function of the projection of the mantelpiece. Rumford fireplaces are permitted to have a firebox depth of 12 in.

For each ⅛-in. projection of a combustible material (drywall or wooden mantelpiece), allow 1 in. of clearance from the fireplace opening, but no matter what the projection you must always have at least 6 in. of clearance. For example, a mantel's jamb that projects 1 in. must be at least 8 in. from the opening.

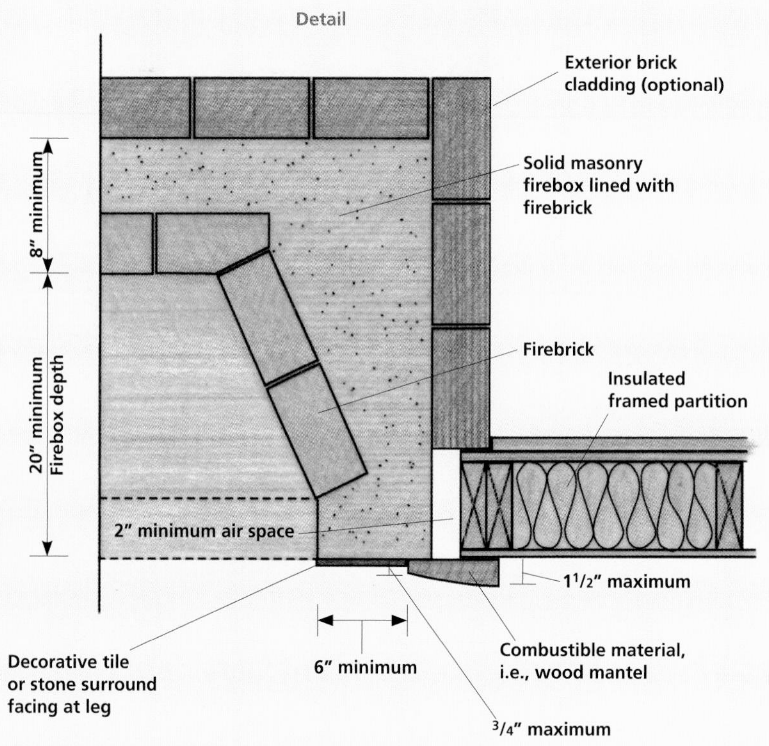

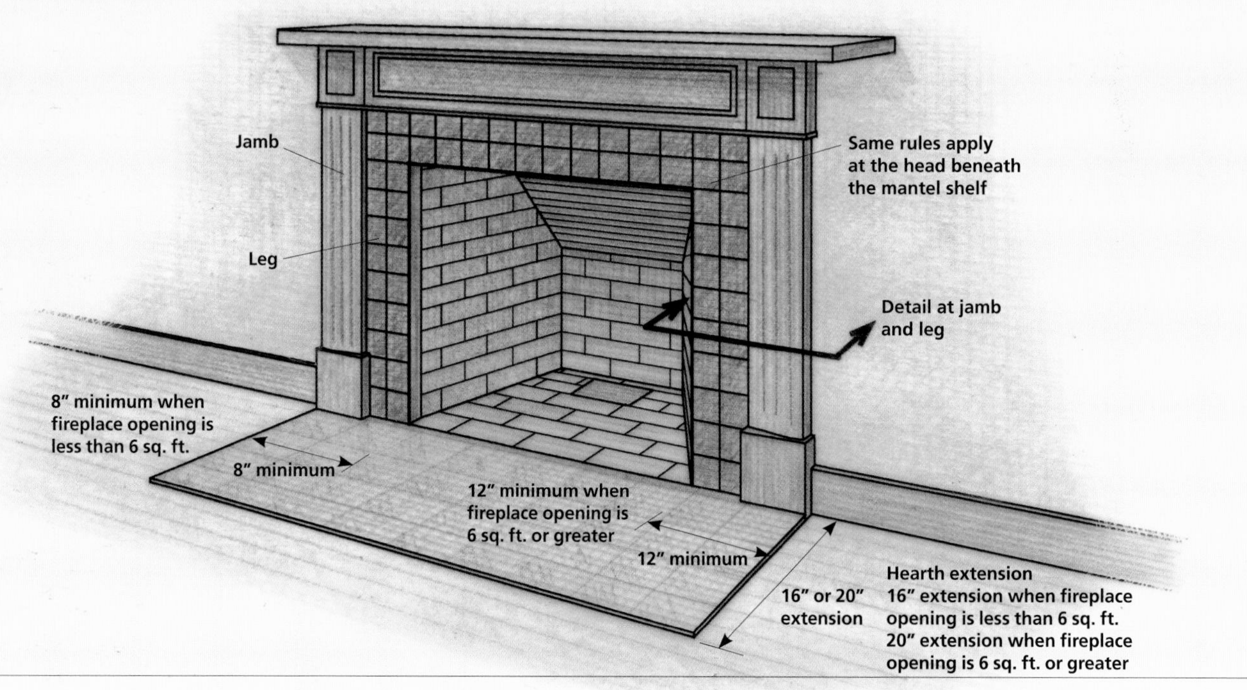

Anatomy of a Traditional Fireplace

Interior view of a fireplace prior to installing decorative surround and mantelpiece

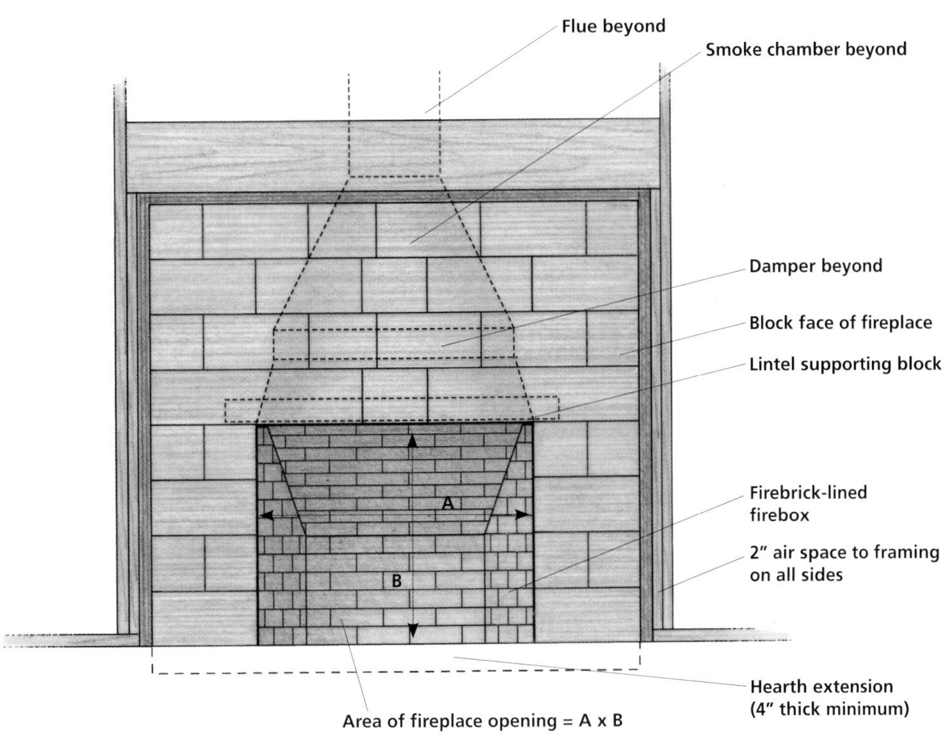

the firebox—where the fire is laid—is constructed out of concrete block, then clad with brick or stone as decorative elements on the outer faces and lined with firebrick on the interior of the firebox.

The Throat and Damper — The walls at the top of the firebox taper upward to a narrow throat that forms the transition between the firebox and the flue. At the throat, a mechanical device called a damper acts as a door to open and shut the pathway to the flue. The damper is opened to let smoke spiral up the chimney while the fire is burning and is closed when there is no fire. Just above the damper is the smoke chamber, an inverted funnel shape at the bottom of the chimney flue that continues to direct smoke up and out. The floor of the smoke chamber just behind the damper is called the smoke shelf, and it prevents any downdraft (smoke or gas that is blown back down the flue from above) from reentering the firebox.

The orientation of the fireplace opening should underscore the architecture. The vertical character of the fireplace draws attention to the height of the room.

THE RUMFORD FIREPLACE

The 18th century brought not only the American Revolution but also a revolution in the way some fireplaces were constructed. Benjamin Thompson, known later as Count Rumford, redesigned the traditional deep fireplace to improve its output of heat and light. He recognized that heat radiates outward, and so built a fireplace with distinctive splayed sides, a tall firebox, and a shallow depth. This was different from the conventional way of constructing fireboxes, which were essentially cubes designed to hold the largest fire possible. Count Rumford also developed a narrow throat that permitted better draw up through the chimney, reducing soot buildup and improving the efficiency of the fire.

Rumford fireplaces are very common in England, because Rumford returned there during the American Revolution. But his designs endured in America as well. Thomas Jefferson employed Rumford-style fireplaces at Monticello. Many older fireplaces were later "Rumfordized" by raising the height of the lintel and adding additional brick within the firebox to create the shallow depth and splayed sides.

Today you can hire artisans who are certified to craft Rumford fireplaces. These are eligible, experienced masons who have taken a course and passed an exam. But a Rumford fireplace isn't necessarily an expensive, labor-intensive venture. You can buy precast throats, dampers, and smoke chambers for site-built Rumford fireplaces, and some manufacturers sell prefabricated components that follow the Rumford design. One such company makes a kit of parts that interlock like toy bricks. Using a crane, a small team of carpenters can stack the pieces and build an entire Rumford fireplace and chimney in a day. Another company offers a steel framework that takes the guesswork out of constructing a Rumford firebox. With the frame in place, a mason can lay block and brick up against it for a perfectly proportioned fireplace.

Anatomy of a Rumford Fireplace

Benjamin Thompson, also known as Count Rumford, calculated precise geometric relationships between fireplace components to create a fireplace with a narrower throat, shallower depth, and taller opening that emitted much more heat than the traditional deep masonry design. The current fireplace building code allows a minimum depth of 12 in. for a Rumford fireplace.

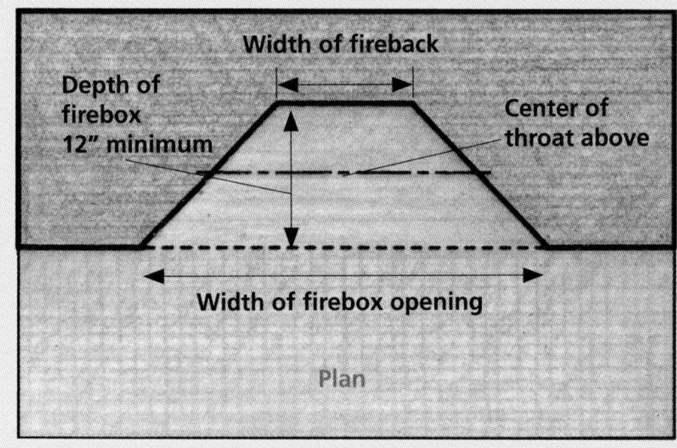

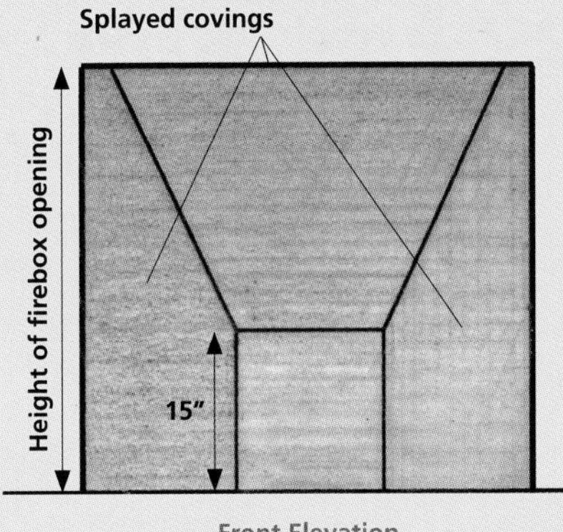

Count Rumford's "Rules"

- **The width of the fireback is equal to the depth of the firebox.**
- **The width of the fireplace opening is equal to three times the depth of the firebox.**
- **The height of the fireplace opening is equal to three times the depth of the firebox.**
- **The center of the throat is exactly above the midpoint of the depth of the firebox.**
- **The throat is never wider than 4".**
- **The forward slope of the fireback begins at 15". above the floor of the hearth.**
- **The vertical distance between the lintel and the smoke shelf is 12".**

Fireside Lore

THE ROSIN FIREPLACE

In 1939, Professor Peter Rosin of Great Britain determined the most aerodynamic shape for a fireplace and chimney. His design eliminated the smoke shelf altogether, creating an undulating rear wall with a pronounced hump that increases radiant heat into the room and directs smoke and gases up the chimney.

Sizing the fireplace opening

Determining just how large or small your new fireplace should be is more of a science than you might think. For example, the fireplace opening, or the void between the mantel and the hearth, and the size of the firebox need to be carefully considered in relation to the size of the room and to each other. There are "standard" sizes that are based on tradition, the dimensions of modular block and brick, and aesthetic preferences. Too large a fireplace for the size of the room might make the room too hot. Build a small fire within that large fireplace, and the fire will be dwarfed by the oversized opening. The Masonry Institute of America suggests these ratios of fireplace opening to room area: for small rooms, 1 to 30, and for larger rooms, 1 to 65. For a den that is 12 ft. by 14 ft., for example, the area of the fireplace should be approximately 5 1/2 sq. ft., or 2 ft. by 2 1/2 ft. For a great room that is 20 ft. by 40 ft., the area of the fireplace opening should be about 12 sq. ft., or 3 ft. by 4 ft.

Once you've established the overall area of the fireplace opening, you can determine what the height-to-width ratio should be and, from that, the corresponding depth. A typical height-to-width ratio of a traditionally sized fireplace is between 1 to 1 and 1 to 2. One exception is the Rumford fireplace, which is proportioned for greater heat radiation. Many fireplace openings end up a close approximation of the golden mean, a ratio based on a Pythagorean proportion of 1 to 1.618. This proportion is found in nature and in man-made forms and seems to be the most aesthetically pleasing proportion.

Traditional, single-faced fireplaces that are a typical 26 in. high by 36 in. wide require an interior depth of at least 20 in., whereas larger fireplaces that are 32 in. high and 48 in. wide require a depth of 25 in. This depth is measured from the inside of the fireplace opening to the face of the firebrick or other refractory materials.

PREFABRICATED FIREPLACES

There are basically two kinds of manufactured fireplaces. The first type is a fireplace insert that is installed within an existing masonry fireplace to improve the heat output and reduce drafts. It is

FACING PAGE: Hefty slabs of granite attach to the block substructure without any visible grout lines. Even irregular masonry units must follow building code requirements for the size of the hearth and firebox opening.

LEFT TOP: The steel damper is manufactured to mount in standard sizes of masonry fireplaces, and it regulates the flow of smoke up the chimney.

LEFT BOTTOM: The horizontal proportion of this custom fireplace accentuates the modern look of the home.

ABOVE: The sides of the metal fireplace are visible through the openings of the sculptural mantelpiece. The fireplace is top vented, but then the flue takes a turn and disappears into the masonry tower behind.

TOP RIGHT: Because prefab fireplaces are inexpensive, more resources can go to custom cabinetry and other niceties. A television is concealed in the cabinet to the left of the fireplace.

BOTTOM RIGHT: Even with a prefab you can design a surround that suits the surroundings. A tile surround dresses up this prefab and makes a romantic view from the bed.

FACING PAGE: Because Rumford fireplaces burn hot and a hot fire produces less creosote, the chimney flue above this Rumford fireplace stays cleaner longer than that of a traditional firebox.

basically a stove tucked into the fireplace recess.

The second type is a prefabricated zero-clearance fireplace, a factory-made steel firebox that allows the fireplace to be installed within a wood-framed enclosure instead of a bulky, costly masonry shell. Most types mimic conventionally built masonry fireplaces. The term "zero clearance" indicates that these units can be installed in very close proximity to combustible material, which is most often wood framing. Manufacturers and code restrictions limit the proximity to 1 in. to 2 in. of air space between the unit and the surrounding framing. The wood framing is susceptible to burning if it comes in contact with the prefab unit. Even relatively low temperatures of 200°F or so can scorch wood. The interior of the prefab's firebox is lined with 1-in.-thick refractory panels that are made of a heat-resistant ceramic material that has been stamped to look like brick.

In general, prefabricated fireplaces are best used for more decorative fireplaces rather than as the sole heat source in a home, because they wear out and the steel shell can deform or crack over time.

Installing a Prefabricated Fireplace

Prefabricated fireplaces are lightweight steel fireboxes that fit into a wood-framed box and connect to a metal flue. Wood-burning versions (shown here) must be vented conventionally upward through a chimney, whereas gas-burning ones can be vented directly through the rear or side wall without a chimney. Once installed, prefabricated fireplaces can be finished with a decorative surround, hearth, and mantelpiece.

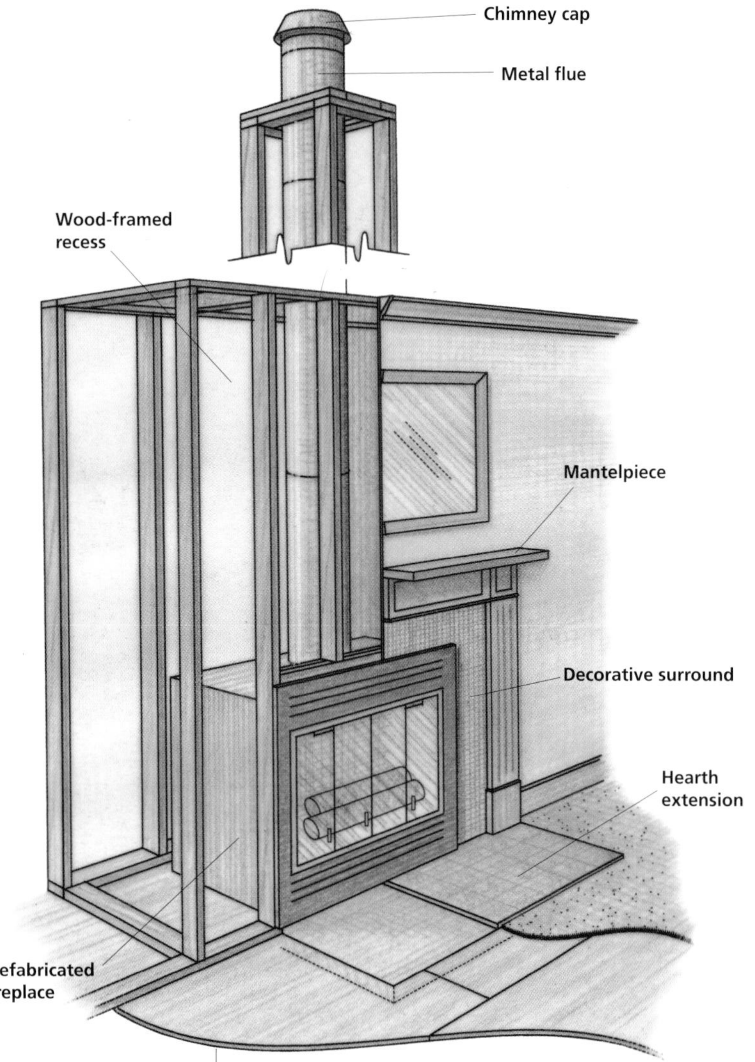

Venting a prefab

Prefabricated fireplaces are vented through a metal flue that can either be encased in a wooden chimney structure that exits up through the roof or be exposed as a decorative element in the room, terminating in a chimney cap above the roof. The flue is a round stainless steel pipe that vents the gas and smoke up through the chimney. Depending on the installation, the flue can be rigid or flexible. All metal flues must meet building code requirements for testing, size, and installation, including review by Underwriters Laboratories (UL®), and receive a certificate that they meet certain standards. There are single-wall, double-wall, and triple-wall metal flues; only Type A double-wall or triple-wall UL-127 flues are permitted for wood-burning fireplace installations.

Installing a prefab

Prefabricated wood-burning fireplaces, metal flues, and component parts are sold as complete systems that must be installed together in order to operate properly. You should employ a certified fireplace specialist—often the fireplace vendor—to install one of these systems, because it is important to follow the manufacturer's installation instructions precisely to ensure proper and safe usage and to guarantee that the applicable state building codes are followed. You'll have no need for a skilled

Certification

The National Fireplace Institute, the certification division of the nonprofit Hearth Education Foundation, is responsible for testing professionals in the fireplace, stove, and chimney industry.

To achieve certification by this agency, applicants have to complete several years of training and take a vigorous exam to demonstrate their knowledge of technique, safety, and building codes in one of three fuel specialties—gas, wood, or pellet. Only after obtaining this qualification may installers, vendors, and designers call themselves NFI Certified Specialists. This certification is not a license but an indication of the specialist's proficiency and professionalism.

FACING PAGE: Exposed stainless steel flues are high tech as well as self-supporting, and this industrial aesthetic suits a more contemporary setting. Their vertical form draws the eye up to the ceiling.

LEFT: This asymmetrical fireplace wall has a slot behind the fireplace for storing logs. The raised hearth, cantilevered off the wall, offers a permanent place to perch.

CREATING NOT SO BIG HOUSE
Susanka

mason if the design of the chimney is all wood, with no applied stone or brick cladding. Prefabs can be added during a renovation in almost any room in the house as long as there is sufficient floor space and a pathway up through the house for an adequate exhaust system. Because they are so light, prefabs don't require as massive a foundation to support their weight as masonry fireplaces do. Some zoning regulations prohibit adding to the footprint of a house, so where a site-built masonry fireplace isn't allowed, a lightweight cantilevered prefab fireplace might be a permissible alternative.

WHERE DOES YOUR FIREPLACE BELONG?

Including a fireplace in our home is rarely a necessity, but nevertheless, given the chance—and the budget—most of us would like to have one, even if we never burn a fire in it. Whether you are planning a fireplace for a newly built home or for an existing home, you must first decide if you want a masonry or a prefabricated unit, because that choice impacts where you can put the fireplace. For those who are planning new construction, including a fireplace in the design is a relatively simple proposition because you can add a masonry or prefabricated unit to any room—and anywhere in the room—if you're planning for it from the start.

When adding a fireplace to a room that never had one before, things can be a bit tricky. You'll need a clear picture in your mind of not only where you want the fireplace to go, but also where the foundation will be poured if you're planning for a masonry fireplace and the path that the chimney will take up through your house. A masonry fireplace, with its wide chimney and substantial foundation, can't be shoehorned into just any place in your house. In general, you might find that the only place for it is on a perimeter wall of the house, because that is the only place you can pour a foundation without disrupting the existing structure. A prefab offers you more flexibility, as it doesn't need a sizeable concrete foundation, but its metal flue still needs a clear vertical path through a shaftway, which will impact the rooms and roof above. Whether masonry or prefab, if the new chimney runs up alongside the house you'll have to make sure that windows on higher floors aren't blocked.

Once you've made the choice between masonry and prefab, the natural inclination is to jump ahead and start shopping for a mantelpiece. But take some time to think carefully about the fireplace's posi-

ABOVE: This fireplace and chimney take center stage as the focal point of the architecture. Their commanding presence is felt even when no fire is burning.

LEFT: A tall, wide chimney would have obscured the view out of the second-floor windows, so instead the chimney narrows down to a thin brick shaftway above the broad back of the fireplace.

FACING PAGE: Prefabricated fireplaces are available in enough variety to fit into any design scheme. Here, the exposed face of the fireplace frame echoes the mantel's copper trim.

ABOVE: A small fireplace can get lost on a long wall, but because this fireplace's face is flush with the wall, the mantel and hearth can extend beyond the stone surround, which visually enlarges the fireplace's composition.

RIGHT: The cozy inglenook at the end of this study creates a symmetrical view of the fireplace and out its flanking windows when seated at the desk.

tion in the room, its size, its orientation to doors and windows, and whether you can comfortably arrange furniture around it. Will it be along a wall or freestanding? Single faced or open on two or more sides? Shelves and cabinetry, extensive paneling, and television wiring will also impact where the fireplace is positioned.

Up against the wall

When thinking about where to locate your fireplace, you can abide by strict rules of symmetry: put the fireplace on center on a wall with equally spaced doors or windows on either side. Or you can look for a more eclectic composition that attractively balances all the elements; for example, place the fireplace off center, extend shelving across the entire wall, and put artwork high up on the other half of the wall for a yin-yang effect. If the fireplace is on an outside wall, it's often nice to put windows on the same wall, so that during the day when the fire isn't burning you'll have a striking view. At night, when the drapes are drawn, the fireplace takes over as the main focal point.

There are two ways to arrange a fireplace relative to the partition that it sits against. "Outies" project the fireplace volume out into the room, occupying floor space and creating recesses to either side.

Storing Wood Indoors

Wood-burning fireplaces and stoves rely on the homeowner to feed them with fuel on a regular basis to keep them burning. Because no one wants to make a trip out to the woodpile on a cold, snowy night, a small quantity of wood is typically kept indoors where it can stay dry and accessible. Depending on how much wood you want close at hand, you can keep a few logs in a log holder that sits on the floor nearby or store much more in a special recess designed alongside the fireplace. Be cautious, however, that you are not bringing in more than just wood. Field mice, snakes, and insects make their homes in stacks of cordwood, and they might be glad to nest in a warm house as well.

The colonists understood the benefit of thermal mass and radiant energy even if they didn't use that vocabulary. Back-to-back and shoulder-to-shoulder fireplaces at the core of the house are most efficient for heating.

"Innies" place most of the mass of the fireplace behind the wall so that no additional floor space is taken up. The fireplace's bulk and chimney can push to the outdoors if the fireplace is on an outer wall, sits within an adjacent recess or closet, or bumps out into the room beyond. In any case, keep in mind that fireplaces take up floor space, whatever their position.

In general, fireplaces that are totally contained within the perimeter of the house burn more efficiently and are able to release more radiant heat into the house from all sides. The air inside the flue remains closer to room temperature, and igniting a fire is easier when you don't have a column of cold air inside the chimney. Locating the fireplace within a house's walls is an important consideration from a budget point of view as well. If the bulk of the chimney is concealed behind interior walls, you'll save on pricey brick or stone cladding. Also, this location may make it easier for the furnace or boiler flue to share the same chimneystack. In any case, one chunky chimney with two flues has more architectural presence than two spindly ones.

Back-to-back fireplaces

When fireplaces are set in the interior of the house you can mimic historical patterns and put separate second or even third fireplaces back to back so that each flue rises up through a common chimney. This is the best arrangement to get the maximum

Paired Fireplaces

Pairing fireplaces within a single chimneystack is the most efficient and economical way to construct two or more masonry fireplaces. Fireplaces that are arranged to sit back to back, side by side, or stacked on top of each other require minimum distances between flues and fireboxes, as dictated by the building code. These drawings illustrate two different arrangements for fireplaces constructed of decorative brick over a solid masonry firebox.

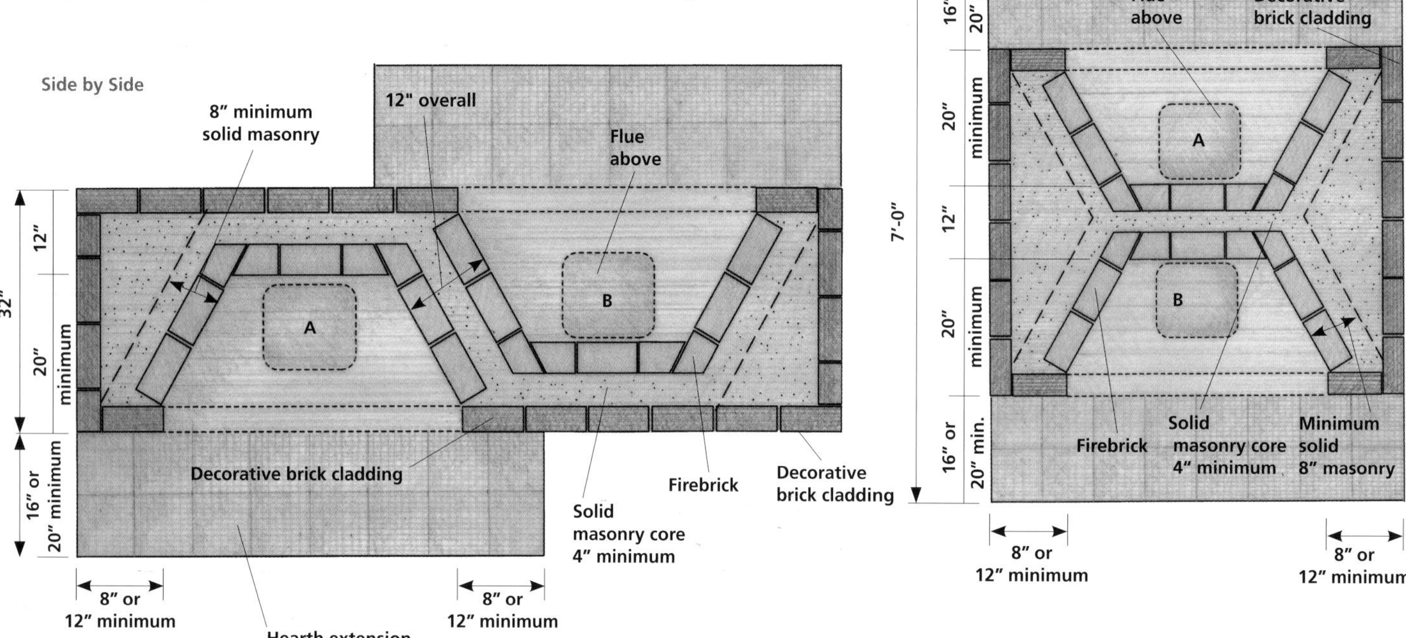

RIGHT: Although this fireplace is in the center of the room, it doesn't dominate the space. The chimney flue is exposed, leaving a broad surface above the firebox for display and a peek across to the dining area.

FACING PAGE TOP: With or without a fire burning in it, this two-sided fireplace creates a framed view through an interior window into the dining room from the seating area beyond.

amount of heat from a masonry fireplace because more of the chimneystack is contained within the envelope of the house and the stored heat can radiate into the house from all sides. This arrangement will certainly impact the floor plan, as its dimen sions are sizable. There are code requirements for the thickness of the walls between back-to-back fireplaces and between adjacent flues, so that at a minimum you'll need 52 in. for back-to-back fireplaces, exclusive of hearths.

One fireplace may have two open faces so that rooms on either side of a wall share the same view of the flames. A see-through fireplace is successful in suites of rooms where you don't mind a little peek through to the other side, like between a master bedroom and master bathroom. Because of the potential hazard for fire to be blown through into one room from the other, it's recommended that fire-resistant glass be placed on one side.

Freestanding fireplaces

Another option is to have the fireplace extend like a peninsula into the room, with two or three open faces. With this arrangement, more of the fire is visible, like an open campfire, so that furniture can be arranged all around it. Most open-sided fireplaces of this configuration are custom built because there are so many design variables for each space. Some prefabricated fireplace manufacturers offer models with more than one open face, but those selections are limited by practical shipping and manufacturing restrictions.

To incorporate a freestanding fireplace, you'll need a large room. This type of fireplace works well in a great room that has both seating and dining areas, because it helps to separate and define the two spaces. But if the fireplace is in the middle the room, make sure that is has enough bulk to assert itself, or it will look lost. Remember that you'll see all sides of it, so think in three dimensions when you are picking out mantelpieces. The back side of the fireplace, on the opposite side of the firebox, will need to be dressed up as well.

With all four sides of a freestanding fireplace exposed, you have the opportunity to open more than one face of the firebox to view for a see-through fireplace.

The Art of Fire

The Chimneystack

The chimneystack of old referred to the entire fireplace and chimney together, and was very large by today's standards. Often three fireplaces radiated out of a single chimneystack on the ground floor, and several more on the floor above added their flues to the stack. The overall dimensions of the stack could easily reach 7 ft. by 10 ft.

These days, chimneys and chimneystacks are considerably slighter. Our houses don't have fireplaces in every room, and fireplaces today are smaller and burn more efficiently, so the surrounding chimney structure has been reduced in size.

On Fire

Kindling Materials

Kindling and newspaper are essential for starting a fire and should be kept close at hand. Fatwood is a type of kindling sold by the bagful in specialty shops. It is made up of small pieces of pine about 8 in. long and less than 1 in. thick. The wood comes from the stumps of pine trees, which contain a high concentration of natural resins. The resins ignite quickly and remain alight, making fatwood a good choice for kindling.

Newspaper is the only kind of household paper that can be used safely in fireplaces and stoves. Coated paper stock, fancy wrapping paper, and paper with colored ink contain pigments or chemicals that may be toxic when burned, so recycle those papers and rely on plentiful newsprint pages. You can crumple newspaper up or make "Nantucket knots": long, loosely rolled tubes of newspaper tied in knots so that they won't uncrumple or roll out of the firebox.

A fireplace for every room

We tend to think of fireplaces being in formal, public rooms like living rooms, libraries, and dens, but more and more fireplaces are cropping up in less predictable spots like dining rooms, kitchens, bedrooms, and even bathrooms. There is no reason not to consider putting a fireplace in any room in your house.

Living Room — The most obvious place to add a fireplace is in a space like the living room or family room, where large groups of people gather. For these rooms, it's important to consider traffic flow, or the path that you'll take moving from one end of the house to the other. The concern is navigating the main seating or activity area that faces the fireplace. If someone is constantly walking past the hearth to get from room to room, it disrupts the spatial connection between your place and the fire's place, and you'll find it awkward and unpleasant to use.

One helpful exercise is to play with different arrangements by cutting out pieces of paper to represent your furniture and the fireplace. Try placing the fireplace on the long wall, the short wall, and even in the corner, then place your furniture around it. Plan on needing between 10 ft. and 14 ft. between the fireplace and the back of the sofa. Any less space than that and you'll feel squished up against it; any farther away and you might as well be in the next room.

Of course, in some homes there just isn't the room for such a sitting area around the fireplace. In that case, you might forego a large facing sofa and place a pair of large armchairs with a shared ottoman on either side of the hearth, which should still allow enough room for traffic flow.

Dining Room — In the dining room, you want your guests to focus on the delicious meal on the dining table, leaving the fireplace as a periphery design element. Dining rooms, if separated from other rooms, tend to be more formally decorated and the mantel is the perfect spot to display our treasures. A fireplace and its surround should match this formal tone. Keep

LEFT: Every fireplace should be as inviting as this one. Its design hearkens back to Colonial-era fireplaces, with the adjacent baker's oven now used as log storage.

BELOW: A fireplace set at the end of a rectangular-shaped room with his and her bookcases on either side invites his and her armchairs out front.

Using the same granite at the hearth, tub deck, and tile wall lends a unifying composition to a small space. The polished surfaces are reflective, so the flames are mirrored in the hearth's surface.

in mind that you'll need 3 ft. to 4 ft. between a blazing fire and the nearest chair or else you'll toast your guest.

Kitchen — In the kitchen, you can place the kitchen table close to the fire, creating a cozy spot for a late-night supper or a relaxed brunch. You may find that a fireplace in the kitchen invites you to linger over meals. If the fireplace serves as both a decorative feature and a pizza oven, it needs to be planned for both purposes so it is convenient to the chef but doesn't get in the way of diners when the chef is baking pies.

Bedroom — Fireplaces in bedrooms tend to be smaller to create an intimate spot for two. It's nice to be able to see the fireplace while you're sitting up in bed reading, so often it is placed opposite the bed wall. If you are burning gas instead of wood, consider prefab models and log sets (more on those in Chapter 5) operated by remote control so you can extinguish the fire as easily as you turn off your bedside lamp.

Master Bath — Taking the romantic notion of tubside candles one step further, some new homes are designed with fireplaces in the

Raising this fireplace off the floor allows the family to enjoy it while eating dinner.

On Fire

Keeping the Fire Burning

To burn properly, a fire needs plenty of oxygen. To supply oxygen to a smoldering fire, you might use a bellows to direct a stream of air into the heart of the log pile in the hearth. Historically, bellows were found in blacksmith shops, where huge accordion-style units, pumped by the smith's apprentice, would blow air into the forge while the smithy made iron implements.

As early as the 14th century it was understood that fires burned better and hotter if they were raised up off the floor of the hearth so that air could circulate all around the burning logs. Fireplace grates—metal grills set off the floor on small legs—allow good airflow. When you use a grate you can also stuff kindling and newspaper under the grate and they won't be crushed by the weight of the logs. Andirons, or firedogs, operate on the same principle. Andirons are metal stands that come in pairs, and most have decorative parts that face the room.

master bathroom. What is more luxurious than toweling off in front of an open fire? Bathrooms with a fireplace are not necessarily extravagant. Prefab fireplaces are good choices for these spots, as they can fit into a smaller area and cost the same as a fancy tub.

CHIMNEY BASICS

Determining the sort of fireplace you'll have and its location is still only part of the job of designing it. The fireplace, after all, is a recess hollowed out of the base of a substantial masonry chimney that extends from the firebox to the sky. This chimney does the job of channeling smoke and gas safely up and out of your house. Wood-burning zero-clearance fireplaces also need to vent smoke safely, although they don't need a masonry chimney. For prefabs, a metal chimney encased in a wood-framed shaft is sufficient. Either way, to properly design your chimney you'll need to understand how it works and why some chimney designs are more appropriate for certain styles of houses (see Chimney Styles on p. 65). When it's designed well, a chimney can unify a home's exterior or add more visual interest.

ABOVE: Fortunate homeowners may find that even their attic spaces were built with working fireplaces. Although attics were traditionally servants' or children's rooms, today these garrets are romantic hideaways.

LEFT: Dining by firelight is an intimate affair and encourages guests to linger at the table. Keep your table far enough away from the hearth so that someone can easily pass and so your guests aren't broiled.

The Art of Fire

Laying a Fire

Simple to learn, years to master. There are basic steps that you can take to lay, ignite, and enjoy a crackling fire. Be sure that your chimney is clean, that the damper is fully opened, and that there are no obstructions. Have all your fire lighting materials nearby. You'll need matches, crumpled newspaper, some small pieces of kindling (softwood works best), and logs. Save the fat pieces for when the fire is fully established; instead, start with thin logs.

- **Crumple newspaper and lay it under the grate or andirons, holding the paper in place with several pieces of kindling.**
- **Place three logs to the rear of the grate or the andirons, stacking them so that there is some airflow between them. If you can, place the logs in a teepee formation to allow even more airflow beneath and around them.**
- **In cold weather, prime the flue by holding a wad of burning newspaper up to the open damper. This will send a current of hot air up the chimney and push the cold air up and out of the way. You'll get a better draft by doing this.**
- **Start the fire by striking a match and putting it to the crumpled newspaper. This should start the combustion process. After your fire is burning well, close the screen for safety.**

Inner workings

Understanding how fireplaces, flues, and chimneys work together to safely vent a fire is vital, especially when planning for a new fireplace. Different layers of materials keep the smoke spiraling up a chimney safely: the flue (the hollow lining that begins at the throat above the firebox), the solid core that supports and protects the flue, and the outer cladding that enhances the architecture.

A proper flue is essential to a fireplace's performance. There are two basic types of flues: ceramic flue tile and metal flue pipe. Ceramic flues come in round, square, or rectangular dimensions and are fabricated in 3-ft. sections. They are stacked and cemented together with heat-resistant refractory mortar. Ceramic flues must be encased in a masonry core, typically concrete block, which is the least expensive material. The concrete chimney core is covered in stucco, overlaid with brick or stone, or clad in metal, depending on the architect's design.

When it comes to prefabricated fireplaces, the round metal flue pipe is part of the system and is commonly encased within wood framing sheathed in plywood. This wooden shaft can be treated with a coat of stucco, faced with brick (to imitate a masonry chimney), clad in thin, synthetic stone material, or sided with wood shingles or clapboard.

MAINTENANCE — Even with proper maintenance, a flue can be cracked or perforated by a chimney fire, coated with a buildup of dangerous amounts of creosote, or damaged by crumbling mortar and

Fireside Lore

CHIMNEY SWEEPS

Far from the image of the cheery sweep in Mary Poppins, sweeps in the 17th through 19th centuries were six-year-old boys whose task it was to shimmy down the flue tied to a rope and clean off the grime. The smaller the better, so sweeps were often underfed.

This chimney appears to have grown out of the earth, like a prehistoric stone tower. The windows alongside it are scribed to follow the taper of the chimney as it rises.

FACING PAGE: Rather than concealing the flue from a fireplace below, this architect chose to celebrate it and highlight it against a large expanse of glass. Some additional heat radiates from the flue—an added bonus.

LEFT: To accommodate a fireplace on a lower floor but not interfere with the home's framing at the ridgeline of the roof, the brick chimney is slanted at the second floor.

broken apart. Older chimneys may have no flue lining at all, relying only on the stone or brick mass of the chimney to direct the smoke and hot gas safely up and out. Yearly inspections and cleaning by a certified chimney sweep will identify any problems.

To improve your chimney's draft and make it safer, you can reline the flue to re-create a smooth passage to expel the smoke and gas. There are two ways to do this: First, a new stainless steel liner can be inserted from the top, either in sections or as a flexible steel hose. This relines the existing ceramic flue. A second technique is to insert an inflatable bladder like a long skinny balloon into the chimney and pour refractory concrete around it. Once the concrete is set, the balloon is collapsed and removed.

Height

For the most effective release of smoke and hot gas, a chimney needs to be long enough to get the proper draw. Hot smoke actually follows a spiral pattern upward, but as wind blows over the top of a chimney it may create a negative effect on the airflow, and smoke can actually blow back down

On Fire

Sweep Services

Virtually any sooty fellow with a cap and a broom can call himself a chimney sweep. To be sure that you are getting proper and safe cleaning of your chimney, inquire if the sweep carries the Certified Chimney Sweep credential from the Chimney Safety Institute of America. Certified sweeps are tested every three years, and must abide by a Chimney Sweep Code of Ethics. Ask to see written confirmation of this or check online at www.csia.org.

into the fireplace. Nearby roofs, trees, and even local weather conditions will also affect the current of smoke.

For good draw, there should be at least 12 ft. of chimney above the damper. A taller chimney can improve the draw even more. There are also mechanical means, like dampers and fans, that can be added to the top of the flue, but they are only as reliable as the person who controls the mechanism.

Chimney tops

It is critical to protect the top of the chimney with a well-maintained chimney cap and flue cap to prevent water from making its way in. The chimney cap is the concrete mortar surface that finishes off the chimney; it is laid snug against the sides of the protruding flue and sloped to shed water. The seam where the cap meets the flue is especially vulnerable and must be caulked and inspected often for cracking.

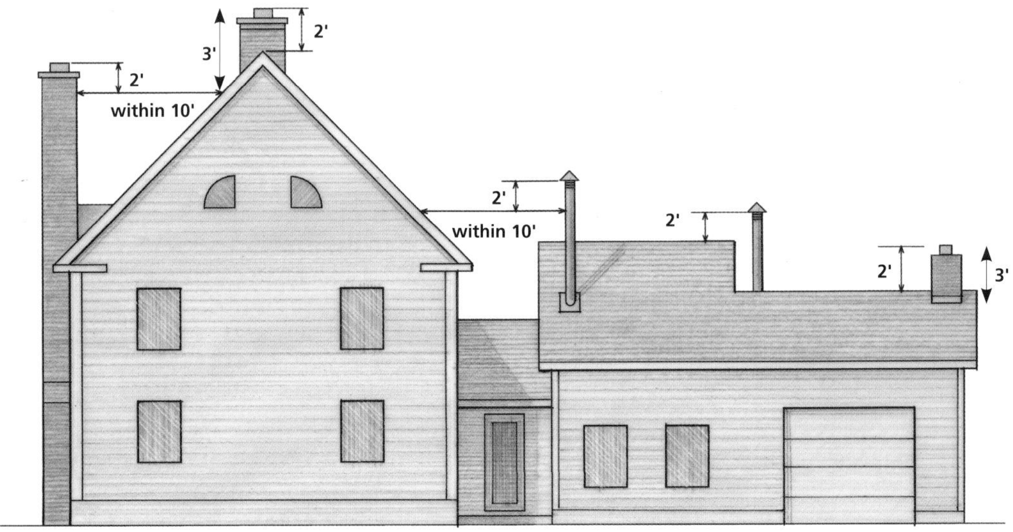

Chimney Heights

Chimneys must extend at least 36 in. above the point at which they exit the roof plane, measured from the "high" side to the top of the flue opening. They must also be at least 24 in. above any nearby point within 10 ft., including parts of nearby buildings. When two or more flues exit from the same chimney, they should vary 4 in. in height to help to decrease downdraft from one flue to the next.

This chimney's height offers a companionable juxtaposition to the tall trees nearby. It is topped by a horizontal roof that helps prevent rain from coming down the flue.

On Fire

Chimney Crickets

Not Jiminy Cricket, a chimney cricket is the bit of extra roof just behind a protruding chimney when the main slope of the roof descends into the backside of the chimney. The ridge of this small roof runs perpendicular to the face of the chimney so that the rain and snow can be shed easily. Mostly chimney crickets are small, only as wide as the chimney is, but the metal flashing that accompanies them is critical to preventing moisture from finding its way into the house.

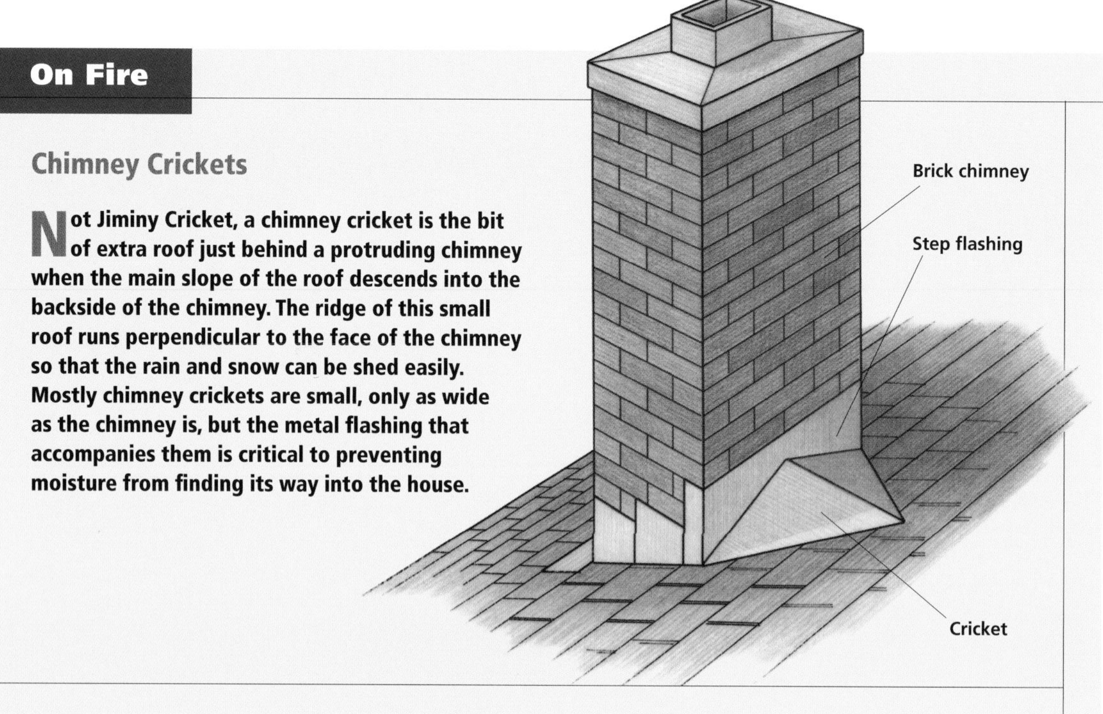

RIGHT: A spark arrester is an easy solution for keeping out unwelcome intruders, like bats and raccoons, as well as rain that could flood the fireplace.

LEFT: A mason carefully caulks the seam between the concrete chimney cap and the protruding ceramic flue. Inspecting its integrity should be a yearly maintenance task to ensure you do not develop a leak in the space between flue and brick.

The flue should extend up past the mortar cap by several inches and also needs to be protected from rain, animals, and debris. One way to do this is to install a spark arrester, which is a metal cage with a solid metal roof that contains flying sparks and keeps out unwanted animal intruders. Another way is to add a horizontal slab of stone supported on masonry legs above the chimney top. This is a more decorative approach, and one that ties into the design of the chimney more successfully than a metal flue cap.

Chimney Pots — A more decorative and more whimsical approach to capping the chimney is to use a chimney pot. Chimney pots date back several centuries, but reached the height of their popularity in Victorian England. They are usually unglazed terra-cotta cylinders that extend the height of the flue. Some chimney pots are colorfully glazed or patterned. Occasionally chimney pots are fashioned of lead-coated copper.

Chimney pots are fastened by mortaring them securely to the flue, and often feature integral hoods that keep the rain from running down inside. Although they are available in various sizes and shapes, most chimney pots resemble chess pieces. Some have charming descriptive names, such as "Pocket Beehives," "Flange Cannon Head," "Grooved Rolls," and "Bellied Pot."

Fireside Lore

Chimney Pot Spotting

Some spot trains, others spot pots. The Central Pot Spotting Authority of Great Britain and Ireland is devoted to the lost art. Enthusiasts seek out unusual chimney pots and score them according to a scheme attributed to a 19th-century Berkshire spotter. Points are awarded to pots with such fanciful names as "Dimbleby Dorrit," "Tadcaster Stoat," and the aptly named "Nobbly Goblin."

Eight chimney pots reveal that eight different fires are burning below in the chimneystack. Chimney pots extend the height of the flue, providing a better draw to the chimney.

CHIMNEY STYLE

Finding the right chimney style and cladding material that looks the best with your house is largely a matter of knowing some rudimentary architectural history and determining your house's style. The right combination of a chimney's placement, shape, and materials will reinforce your home's style and add curb appeal. Navigating through the options can be confusing, so working with a knowledgeable designer or architect to guide you through the process will help you get the right style and stay on budget.

Before you consult a pro, consider some design basics, like where your house fits in the architectural timeline. Your house might be a copy of an 18th-century New England manor house, a Midwestern farmhouse built 100 years ago, or a 1960s ranch house. Being sensitive to its vintage is important, especially in a historic home. An ill-chosen chimney design detracts from the home's character and value, whereas a carefully designed chimney will enhance both. In each case there are historical precedents that will help you choose the chimney accordingly. Many historic styles persist today in newly built homes, and selecting the correct chimney will add authenticity.

Symmetry in brick

Early Colonial-era fireplaces were more indispensable pieces of equipment than architectural features. Fireplaces were located for utility—cooking and heating—and builders were less

RIGHT: This chimney is a natural extension of the stone foundation, but it evolves into a smooth-faced chimney as it penetrates the eave line. An outdoor fireplace is built into the bottom of the chimney as an added bonus.

BELOW: A brick chimney rising out of the roof is such a familiar part of the silhouette of a house that we often overlook the artistry of the bricklayer's work. Spark arresters mounted at the tops of the flues keep embers in and critters out.

FACING PAGE: A ceramic chimney pot punctuates the top of this stone chimney like an exclamation point.

concerned about aesthetics of symmetry or balance than they were about ease of construction. Brick was the material of choice for chimneys, and although architectural flourishes and ornament were not a priority, masons expressed the artistry of their craft in the placement of each brick.

Larger houses of the 18th century had more rooms and robust chimneys that ran up the gable wall, hinting at the deep, boxy fireplaces within. As fireplaces became taller and shallower in dimension to reflect the Count Rumford style, chimneys were incorporated into the perimeter wall of the house, as the firebox was not as sizeable.

From the 1740s to the mid 1800s, popular architectural styles evolved, including Georgian, Federalist, and Greek Revival. In each of these solidly symmetrical styles the chimneys were often sober brick towers that rose straight up without any taper or flourish. In some instances the sole concession to decorative detail was a few courses of corbelled brick at the top or a cast-stone cap.

Brick chimneys are ubiquitous, and often it isn't until we spot an artful one that we recognize the potential for a unique or custom design.

Fireside Lore

CATTED CHIMNEYS

The earliest 17th-century chimneys, known as catted chimneys, were constructed of a heavy timber frame packed with clay. This construction, combined with typical thatched roofs, created a fire hazard. Colonists appointed a "chimney viewer," an individual whose job it was to inspect chimneys for safety. Sadly, few if any of this chimney type remain due to their fragile nature.

Today, simple brick chimneys continue to be paired with ever-popular Colonial and Greek Revival homes because this authentic look is an affordable one as well. Much of the cost of using brick is in the labor to install it, so you can save money by using king-size brick to face your chimney. You can also dispense with brick cladding and instead apply stucco over the chimney's concrete block substructure or plywood sheathing. Stucco can be tinted or painted, and is a long-lasting alternative that suits a traditional home.

If your home is an actual antique or a reproduction, brick is still a good choice, especially if the house's foundation is faced with brick or you've used brick pavers for a walkway or patio. For an authentic look, use handmade brick and give the chimney top some added detail by corbelling the bricks. Brick color is regional, based on the pigments in the local clay beds, so stick to colors representative of historic buildings in your region and steer clear of oversize or king-size bricks on a very small house.

Asymmetry and craft

At the turn of the 19th century the advent of balloon framing freed houses from the boxy shape of timber-framed homes and ushered in more inventive shapes and forms. By the end of the Civil War, architects and designers looked to Europe rather than ancient Greece for inspiration. They borrowed ideas from medieval dwellings, Italian villas, and French chateaux and combined these elements in new and inventive ways. With the introduction of far less rigidly symmetrical architectural styles in the latter half of the 19th century, architects began to incorporate the chimney into more fanciful and varied designs, reflecting the casual, open arrangement of the rooms that balloon framing made possible.

No single architectural style is emblematic of the entire 19th century, but craftsmanship and innovation were important no matter what the style. During this long period, which witnessed the many varieties of Victorian style as well as a range of eclectic, revival, and neoclassical styles, much residential design was based on a picturesque and romantic ideal. Chimneys became taller and often featured unusual patterns and shapes, and even chimney pots, to

Fire Bricks

Fire bricks, or refractory bricks, are specially fabricated bricks for use in high-heat locations. They are designed to withstand temperatures of up to 2,000°F without degradation (a wood fire burns at about 1,500°F). Fire bricks measure 2½ in. by 4 in. by 9 in. and may be laid in decorative patterns like herringbone, stacked bond, and running bond. Refractory panels, which are larger and are found in the fireboxes of prefabricated fireplaces, have brick patterns molded into them so that they look more realistic.

liven them up. No longer just functional smokestacks, they harmonized with the design of the house, reinforcing the style and adding character. The palette of chimney materials was restricted to stucco, brick, and stone, but even in that limited range there was endless variety in composition.

Victorian styles such as Stick and Queen Anne emphasized height, with steeply sloped roofs and tall, delicate chimneys ornamented with undulating brick patterns that created vertical and horizontal bands of shadow and light on the chimney's surface. Victorians used a lot of color on the exteriors of their homes, and this included using a variety of brick colors as well.

In Tudor and Shingle style homes, popular at the end of the 19th century and into the 20th century, the chimney is a signature element that epitomizes the period. The prominently placed, massive

Copper cladding suits the Craftsman aesthetic of this cottage in the woods. The copper is also a good choice of impermeable material to go alongside the outdoor shower.

Like an illustration out of a fairy tale, this chimney gets its unique look from the imperfectly formed clinker bricks that show through the stucco finish.

chimney is often faced with the same material as the foundation wall, reinforcing the link between earth and sky. Large, roughly textured stones were typically laid in an irregular pattern to emphasize the handmade, organic style of the house. Bricks can also have a handmade rather than a precise look, especially when laid with a mixture of colors for a mottled appearance. In some Tudor style homes the fireplace and chimney are on the front façade alongside a cross gable. This look is sometimes referred to as a "storybook," especially when the chimney is faced in a mixture of stone and brick.

20th-century style

By the 20th century, the domestic architectural landscape was an assortment of many styles—some regional, some revivals of earlier Colonial styles, some eclectic, and some imported from abroad. The emergence of a sizeable middle class resulted in the growth of housing developments with modestly sized homes for the growing number of families. In each type of home, the chimney style is a trademark detail.

In the western states, some houses followed a Spanish Colonial model, featuring adobe chimneys clad with stucco and elaborate chimney tops, some with small tile roofs imitating little bell towers. The Craftsman style or bungalow home also originated in the West, in southern California, and one of the hallmarks of this style is the natural stone chimney that tapers up from a broad base, flanked by a window on either side. Tapestry brick that is deliberately roughened during its manufacture was also a popular chimney material for bungalows, particularly when accented with clinkers, or irregular bricks. The Prairie style homes of the Midwest had very wide brick chimneys, not excessively tall, to enhance the horizontal lines of the house style. They featured 12-in. Roman bricks rather than standard 8-in. bricks to emphasize those long, level lines, and repeated the look in the interior as well.

The Bauhaus influence from Europe introduced the International style to America. This style included starkly modern houses with smooth planar surfaces and ribbon windows, and even today these homes look cutting edge. In keeping with the philosophy that houses are "machines for living," chimneys were pared down to white smokestacks or simple stucco shafts. At the same time, other architects built unique modern homes that interpreted vernacular forms and materials in a new way. Stone

ABOVE: Although not symmetrical, there is nevertheless a balanced composition to this elevation, where the metal chimney flue rises skyward from the straightforward concrete block fireplace. Behind the small door is log storage, accessible from inside.

FACING PAGE: This chimney and roofline connect like a bow and arrow. There is a pleasing tension between the verticality of the chimney and the angularity of the roof.

and brick chimneys remained popular, but were sometimes placed in the center of the house with the masonry exposed instead of hidden behind walls and mantelpieces.

The large housing developments built in the mid-20th century pared down middle-class housing to the bare essentials, and the television, not the hearth, was the focus of family gatherings. Chimneys were costly and time consuming to build and did not necessarily increase the value of the house, so many homes did not include fireplaces.

Today, fortunately, fireplaces have regained their prominence in new homes and are being added to those without fireplaces. Once again, people are recognizing and appreciating the aesthetic and monetary value a well-designed and well-constructed fireplace and chimney offer.

Fireside Lore

The Tory Stripe

The "Tory Stripe" is the black stripe found at the top of some Colonial-era white-painted brick chimneys. According to folklore, it identified the homes of British Loyalists, or Tories. Historians say these stripes didn't actually appear on houses until long after the war and really had a more practical purpose: concealing soot and protecting the brick.

126

"Mantels are a signature element of a home's interior design."

CHAPTER

3

Mantelpiece Style: The Mantel, Surround, and Hearth

TODAY WE REFER TO A CHIMNEYPIECE AS THE ORNAMENTAL CONSTRUCTION AROUND A FIREPLACE THAT INCLUDES THE MANTEL, BUT CENTURIES AGO CHIMNEYPIECES WERE UTILITARIAN FIXTURES DIRECTING SMOKE, SUPPORTING COOKING UTENSILS, AND CREATING ALCOVES FOR WARMTH. WITH ADVANCES IN CHIMNEY DESIGN, COOKERY, AND CENTRAL HEATING, CHIMNEYPIECES HAVE GONE THE WAY OF OPERABLE WINDOW SHUTTERS AND ROOT CELLARS. WE STILL HAVE CHIMNEYPIECES, BUT THEY HAVE ASSUMED A DIFFERENT ROLE. WHEN WE SPEAK OF THE CHIMNEYPIECE,WE OFTEN THINK first of the most prominent part, the mantel, which is where we'll focus our discussion in this chapter. Mantels, or mantelpieces, are a signature element of a home's interior design, pronouncing its character and accentuating its vintage. A mantelpiece may reveal your own tastes, hopefully telling as much about your preferences as it does about the style of your house. Whether you adorn your mantel with family photos or a valuable painting, it's where you have the greatest opportunity to make a style statement about your fireplace.

Replacing an old or designing a new mantelpiece presents a challenge and an opportunity. If you're lucky, the mantelpieces in your home are outfitted to your liking: stylistically appropriate for the architectural design of the house, proportioned accurately to the scale of the room, and created with materials and colors that suit the décor.

Mantelpieces assume many forms, from simple wooden shelves to elaborately carved arrangements of stone or plaster. Some fireplaces have no mantelpieces at all, either exposing the masonry structure, or chimney breast, or extending stone or brick cladding across the entire face of the fireplace

FACING PAGE: Paired wall sconces set on a dimmer switch illuminate the objects on the mantel and add a homier feel than a recessed spotlight.

LEFT: The mantelpiece is a stage as much as a shrine, and we put objects that are meaningful to us and our families on the mantel, for display as well as to show that we cherish them. Treasures and antiques like this antique pull toy add an especially personal touch.

FACING PAGE: In early American fireplaces the mantel was synonymous with the lintel, the timber spanning the top of the fireplace opening. Antique versions are frequently scarred with multiple nails and hooks that were used for drying herbs and suspending pots.

RIGHT: Achieving a balance of styles relies on good design. Here, the abstract painting echoes the veins in the antique marble used for the fireplace, tying together seemingly disparate decorative elements.

BELOW: In this Arts and Crafts style home, the mantelpiece is integrated with the trim, and the overmantel is painted with a woodsy scene in keeping with the room's naturalistic flavor.

wall. Metal and concrete have more recently been used in creative ways as well. Mantelpieces may incorporate the entire surface of the wall into the design, with extensive paneling, shelving, and even benches. Generally speaking, a mantelpiece should accentuate the architectural style of the room, whether it is in a Georgian mansion or a Craftsman bungalow.

FIREPLACE STYLE

Part of the pleasure of having a fireplace is designing or updating the mantelpiece to enhance the interior design of your home. The mantelpiece, with all its parts, is a key component of the personality of your home, establishing its style and setting the scene for furnishings and accessories. Usually a fireplace design is coordinated to follow the architectural style of a house, so that the inside follows the outside's lead. But a fireplace doesn't always match a house's architectural style. In fact, some of the more successful and interesting installations are a study in contrast: a starkly modern fireplace in a historic house or an antique mantelpiece in a very contemporary one. The key is to relate the materials and dimensions of the mantelpiece to the house by using compatible masonry, wood, or tile and taking cues from the house's scale and proportions.

Early American

Fireplaces in colonial America were immense in size, because they did double duty as the prime source of heat in the house and as the site for all the cooking and baking. Fortunately, these immigrants had a huge supply of wood at their disposal. The early colonists from Europe constructed fireplaces adapted from the patterns that they brought from home.

English — The English who settled in New England built their fireplaces with massive oak timbers spanning the top of the opening to support the brick chimney breast above. Today we call these structural timbers lintels, but the colonists referred to them as mantels. They protruded slightly off the face of the brick, creating a narrow shelf for candlesticks and small utensils. This mantel was studded with pegs, hooks, and brackets used for suspending pots, drying herbs and linens, and holding implements.

RIGHT: The fireplace carries importance in this dining room, as noted by the white mantel that sets it off from the surrounding paneling and the inlay in the wood floor

BELOW: The designer of this fireplace took as much care in decorating the interior as the exterior faces. Cast iron covers the covings (angled sides) as well as the rear of the firebox to protect the brick and reflect the heat into the room.

Its proximity to the flames meant the mantel was often scorched. To prevent this, though not always successfully, clay mortar was applied to the mantel's underside. Baking was done in built-in ovens, which were first located within the recess of the firebox, which was dangerous to women in long skirts. Later, ovens were built alongside the main fireplace openings and heated by separate fireboxes below.

Dutch — The Dutch, who inhabited the mid-colonies of New York, New Jersey, and Pennsylvania, were skilled bricklayers. Their fireplaces were based on a medieval design, with an open, three-sided hearth that backed onto an exterior brick wall and a chimney supported by massive timber beams above. These fireplaces are sometimes referred to as "jambless," as there were no supporting side walls other than small projections decorated with characteristic blue and white Delft tiles brought over from the old country. Additional tile or an iron fireback helped to reflect the heat out into the room and protected the rear wall. A hood made of boards or short lengths of cloth surrounded the bottom of the chimney to vent the smoke. There were no built-in baking ovens; baking was done in iron pans set among the embers of the hearth.

Other influences from abroad

By the mid-18th century, many new homes were built according to pattern books imported from England featuring what we now call Georgian style architecture. Preexisting homes were updated as well to demonstrate the wealth and growing sophistication of the owners. As houses grew bigger, the kitchen, with its immense utilitarian fireplace, was increasingly segregated from the other, more public or formal family spaces. The kitchen in southern homes likely occupied a separate building to

As architectural influences from abroad came more into vogue, exterior details could be seen inside the home. Here, neoclassical columns and dentil molding decorate a formal fireplace.

keep heat and cooking smells far from the rest of the house. The remaining fireplaces took on a more prominent role in interior design, and mantelpieces in bedchambers, parlors, and dining rooms became more ornate to express the wealth of their owners.

By this time, the wood paneling that originally covered interior walls was replaced with plaster, except at the wainscot—the lower portion of the walls—and the entire fireplace wall in middle-class homes. Sometimes a painting of a landscape would be applied directly on the central panel above the fireplace or a portrait would be hung in this place of pride, flanked by candles in wall-mounted sconces.

Styles from the 18th and 19th centuries

Mantelpieces were designed to emulate miniature building facades, with the firebox opening as the main portal, and were embellished with architectural details taken from the various prevalent classical and neoclassical styles of the 18th century and

Mirrors and carved woodwork gracing the overmantel are some of the hallmarks of fireplaces in Victorian-era homes for displaying collections and photographs within with the mantelpiece's carved "splendor."

on into the first half of the 19th century. Mantelpieces became quite decorative, copying classical ornamental features like dentil molding and elaborate pediments adapted from doorways of Georgian style buildings.

The neoclassical Federal period ushered in a more restrained aesthetic, and mantels had simpler, more graceful details. Ornaments made of plaster or wood depicting urns, swags, or garlands decorated the frieze panel, as well as sunburst motifs. Marble mantels and decorative ceramic tiles were shipped over from Europe to decorate the homes of the well-to-do. Less affluent homeowners employed artisans to apply faux painting on wood to imitate marble. By the middle of the 19th century, mantelpiece compositions included elements from Greek Revival styles—jambs resembled columns and the mantelshelf the broad lintel of a Greek temple.

The turn of the century

The 19th century introduced a less formal aesthetic to home design and to interior design in particular. The concepts of physical ease and spending leisure time in one's home became more important than they were during the more sober and formal

LEFT: Furniture or fireplace? This ornate Victorian-era mantelpiece includes bookshelves, display shelves, and cabinets to satisfy the need to display mementos.

18th century. Furnishings and interior design reflected this attitude. The fireplace, with its decorative mantelpiece, remained in the role of architectural centerpiece and gained status as the emblem of family life.

The Victorian period is notable for its emphasis on abundant decoration, and mantelpieces were no exception. They became increasingly larger and even more ornate. Borrowing and mixing multiple elements derived from the Medieval, Renaissance, and Gothic eras, they included heavily embellished overmantels with built-in shelves.

The Arts and Crafts Influence — The end of the 19th century coincided with the widespread use of coal- or wood-fired furnaces for central heating systems, except in very rural areas. As a result, fireplaces and their mantelpieces shed their functional duty and took on an even more

BELOW: Handicraft and organic hues were emphasized in Arts and Crafts fireplaces. Here extensive tilework complements the simple wood mantel shelves.

INGLENOOKS

An inglenook is an architectural term for a room within a room. Historically, they derived from the side walls and oversize hoods that flanked the great fireplaces in medieval halls. These adjoining walls helped to contain the heat within a smaller area, and this "chimney corner" became the best seat in the house on a cold day. Benches were brought in so that you could sit comfortably within the chimney corner, and this is where the lord and lady would cozy up with their friends on a frigid night.

This notion of a snug room within a room is still popular, and inglenooks are typically found in Craftsman style homes, with wooden benches flanking the fireplace.

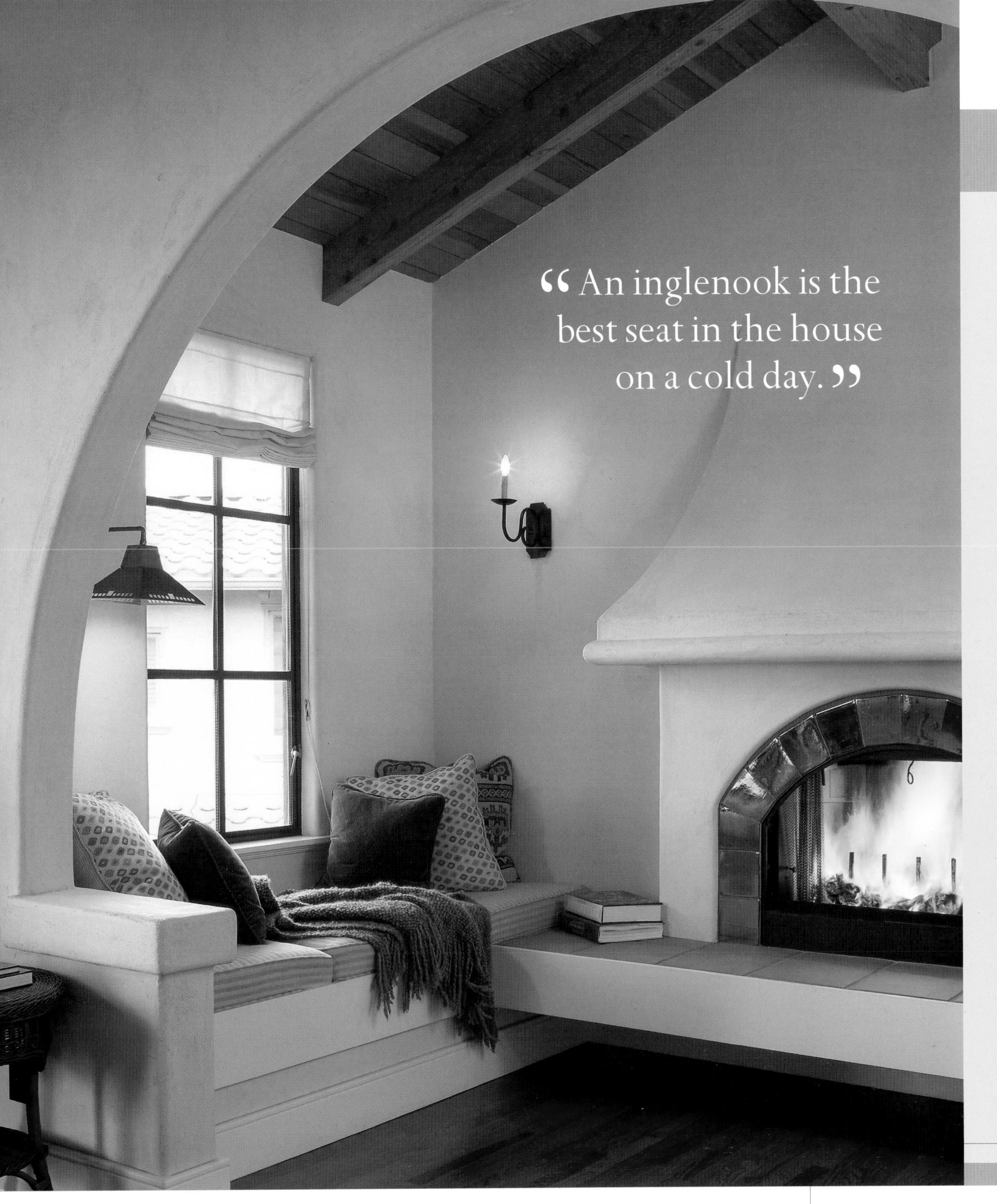
“ An inglenook is the
best seat in the house
on a cold day. ”

symbolic role, where the home's cheerful hearth represented family, domesticity, and prosperity.

The Arts and Crafts movement that emerged before the turn of the century in England reverberated in America as well. The emerging Arts and Crafts aesthetic was a reaction to superfluous ornament and stressed an honesty of materials and handcrafted construction. Ceramic tile, designed and fabricated by Henry Chapman Mercer in the East and Ernest Batchelder in the West, was sought after for its natural hue and handmade quality. Where ceramic tile was used sparingly in the Victorian era, some Arts and Crafts style fireplaces were more liberal in its use, with tile covering the entire mantel and hearth as well.

Eclectic and modern

By the 1920s, architectural fashions followed no one straight course. Termed "Eclectic Revival," the style included Neo-Tudor, Colonial Revival, Spanish Revival, and other variations of earlier centuries' styles. Mantelpieces coordinated stylistically with the design of homes and remained prominent ornamental interior design features.

Frank Lloyd Wright, among many others, reevaluated the concept of home and designed houses that even today we would consider contemporary. Fireplaces were no longer representative of design that had come before, but were reinvented forms, massive structures of brick and stone often freed from the adjacent walls. These fireplaces had mantels like no one had ever seen before—if they even had them at all. Wright, in particular, regarded the fireplace and chimney as the spiritual and ceremonial core of the house, an idea borrowed and adapted from traditional Japanese architecture.

In the wake of the Second World War, enormous housing developments were rapidly constructed to accommodate the subsequent population boom. These starter homes were built fast and cheaply and did not necessarily have fireplaces. Fortunately, in suburban neighborhoods with larger homes, fireplaces were still included in the 1950s, even though by then television sets had emerged as the primary focal points in living rooms and family rooms, eclipsing fireplaces.

These days we yearn once more to have fireplaces. Part of this is the universal craving for a tangible sense of "home," which has spurred manufacturers to develop relatively affordable alternatives, like prefabricated fireplaces.

ABOVE: Richard Neutra, a former partner of Frank Lloyd Wright who worked in California in the first half of the 20th century, designed this fireplace. It is as contemporary today as it was nearly 80 years ago.

LEFT: A folk-art fireplace decorated with dozens of mussel shells frames the unusually shaped brick firebox.

FACING PAGE: The simplest mantel shelf is a timber mounted onto the stone chimneybreast. Colonial fireplaces used such shelves for storing cookware; we use our mantel shelves as miniature galleries for arranging collections and propping art work.

IRORI AND KIVA FIREPLACES

Beyond conventional European style fireplaces, other types of wood-burning fireplaces have made it into our homes and reflect vernacular design forms from the Far East and the American Southwest.

Traditional Japanese farmhouses had an open hearth, or *irori,* in the center of the kitchen for cooking meals and curing meat and fish. These *irori* were square pits surrounded on four sides by a wooden curb. Overhead, a wooden rack held hooks for drying the meat and fish, and a long chain hung down from the ceiling with a large fishhook upon which an iron kettle was hung. Smoke found its way up and out through natural convection, although not particularly well, leading to blackened walls and the ever-present danger of fire to the home. Widespread use of *irori* was ultimately abandoned when electricity came to rural Japan, yet *irori* remain traditional gathering places. Their time-honored design has been modified for installation in modern-day homes.

Adobe fireplaces, known as kiva fireplaces, are synonymous with Southwestern style in home design. The name is taken from the word for the private subterranean chamber used by Pueblo Indian men for religious rites and social meetings. In a traditional kiva fireplace, the opening has a distinctive arched shape that mimics the portal to the kiva chamber, which represents the entrance to the spiritual world and the place from which life came into the earthly world. Kiva fireplaces are traditionally located in corners and fabricated from the same adobe as the house. Often they have built-in benches alongside, as well as small niches for displaying religious icons.

“*Irori* are traditional gathering places, and their design has been modified for today’s homes.”

The Mantelpiece

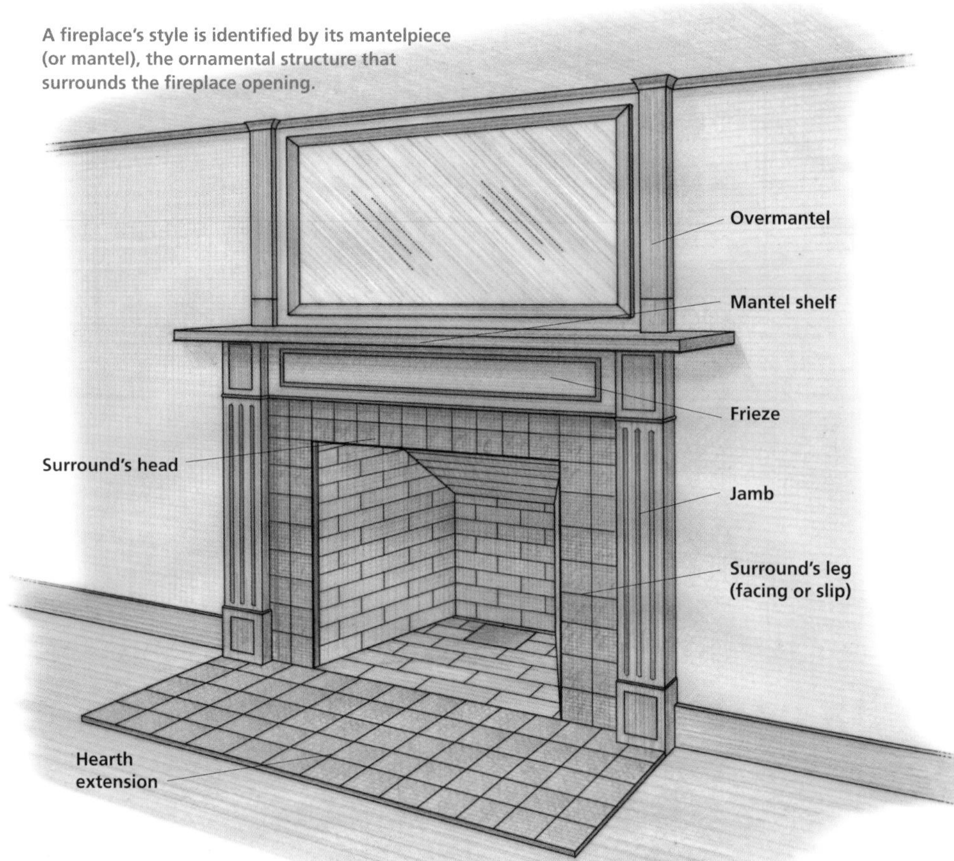

You can achieve an eclectic look by mixing various styles. Here, a formal mantelpiece and custom-painted frieze dress up a prefabricated gas fireplace.

A GLOSSARY OF TERMS

The original meaning of the word mantel referred specifically to the length of wood or single large stone that supported the masonry above the fireplace, that which is now called a lintel. Generally, mantel is shorthand for mantelpiece, the entire arrangement, whether it is a single shelf or a collection of components.

Mantel shelf and jambs

In the simplest configuration of a mantelpiece, a plain wooden board, split log, or single slab of stone is fastened to the chimneybreast (the exposed outer face of the chimney just above the fireplace opening) to form the mantel shelf. More elaborate mantel shelves are supported on decorative brackets or rest on vertical jambs that reach to the floor on either side of the fireplace. Jambs are like miniature pilasters, which are square or round columns that can appear to be embedded into the wall to hold up the mantel shelf.

LEFT: The metal cooktop hood and the fireplace hood are rustic accents in this open, contemporary style home. Their juxtaposition shows how the old idea of a hood to contain smoke can be reinterpreted for today's domestic use.

BELOW: This handsome custom overmantel rises to the two-story ceiling. Pierced wood detailing is repeated throughout the house on other trim, unifying the design of the home.

With many traditional fireplaces, located just below the mantel shelf and between the jambs is the frieze, a flat panel above the fireplace opening. Friezes are often plain surfaces, or they can be ornamented with scrollwork or carvings. Some friezes are narrow and only serve as mounting plates for the mantel's brackets, whereas others are very wide, representing key design elements.

An overmantel is the decorative arrangement of cabinetry and paneling that may sit on or above a mantel shelf against the chimneybreast. Overmantels can be very ornate, incorporating mirrors, light fixtures, and shelves, to function more like a piece of furniture than an element of the architecture. Other overmantels dispense with storage and are instead far simpler paneled arrangements above the fireplace opening.

Some fireplaces do not have the conventional mantel arrangement, and instead sport fireplace hoods. Hoods are wood or metal shapes that are affixed to the face of the chimneybreast and flare

Mantelpiece Glimpses

Zeroing in on a mantelpiece's details is enough to hint at the period and decorative style of the room, and a well-designed mantel will reinforce that style with appropriate forms and materials.

TOP LEFT: The painted mantel and classic entablature with its delicate jamb and ornamented frieze is a sure indication that this formal-looking mantelpiece is in an historic or traditionally designed home.

LEFT: The repetitive blocks under the mantel shelf, the use of hand-made tile in earthy colors, and the naturally finished wood surfaces all reflect the Arts and Crafts style.

TOP RIGHT: This mantel shelf has elements of Arts and Crafts style in the way the shelf is bracketed, but the stone cladding on the fireplace contributes a more substantial and rustic look, appropriate to a two-story family room.

BOTTOM RIGHT: Stainless-steel brackets, sleek lines, and minimalist detailing are a sure bet that this mantelpiece is in a modern home. The industrial nature of the bracket is softened by its graceful construction and its proximity to warm wood paneling and a limestone surround.

You can achieve a unique fireplace surround by working with a local artist. Here, handmade ceramic oak leaves dance around the firebox opening.

out over the top of the firebox. They usually do not have a mantel shelf and are often made of some decorative material, especially metal. Their original purpose was to keep smoke from a blazing fire from entering into the room, and this is why they tended to protrude into the space above the hearth. Today, with better-engineered fireplaces, a hood is more of a decorative feature.

Surrounds

Between the mantel and the firebox opening is a narrow space, referred to as the fireplace's surround, the front-facing portion of the brick or block that forms the firebox. Frequently a finished, decorative material like tile or stone covers the rough brick or block surround. In some cases a more finished brick is used to build the fireplace's front-facing portions, and is meant to be left exposed.

A surround must be at least 6 in. by code on all three sides. Also, it must be comprised of a noncombustible material, and so we often see tile, brick, glass, stone, or other fireproof materials used here. The surround also presents an opportunity to add some individuality to a fireplace, which may have an off-the-shelf mantel in need of some pizzazz.

The size and proportion of the fireplace opening will influence the width of the surround's head and legs, or top and side portions, but don't be limited by the code minimums. A taller head and wider legs will visually enlarge the size of your fireplace and in turn permit you to install a larger mantelpiece.

FACING PAGE: The tall stones that crown the lintel of this stone fireplace appear to extend the overall height of the fireplace's opening. Each stone was hand fit by a master mason.

LEFT: This hearth is bounded by a patterned inlay that extends past the firebox opening. Small touches add a dainty detail in contrast to this fireplace's massive stones.

Hearth

The decorative parts of a mantelpiece aren't restricted to mantel shelves and tile surrounds. The hearth, or the floor of the fireplace, is another place to add style and substance to the design. By code, that portion of the hearth that extends out beyond the face of the fireplace, the hearth extension, must be easily distinguishable from the adjacent flooring, and that is an invitation to install decorative stone, brick, or tile to contrast a wooden or carpeted floor. Hearths are required for all wood-burning fireplaces to reduce the risk of fire. A gas fireplace does not require a hearth extension, although it looks more like an authentic wood-burning fireplace when it has one.

Fireside Lore

CRICKET ON THE HEARTH

Charles Dickens's story "The Cricket on the Hearth" is based on the folklore that when a cricket makes its way into your house and takes up residence in your fireplace, it brings good luck.

RIGHT: The three sections of this colorful surround were made by inserting small glazed tiles and broken pieces of crockery into a matrix of epoxy within a mold.

BELOW: Clinker bricks, so named for the sound they make when they are banged together, add color to this multidimensional fireplace design. Craftsman style homes used clinker bricks for their handmade look and charming irregularity.

For safety reasons the minimum size of a hearth extension is governed by the building code, and its dimensions are determined according to the area of the fireplace opening. For a fireplace less than 6 ft. in area the hearth extension must be at least 16 in. deep from the face of the opening and must extend 8 in. to either side of the opening. Fireplace openings that are 6 ft. or more in area require that the hearth be 20 in. deep and extend 12 in. beyond the sides of the opening.

Brick, stone, ceramic tile, metal, or concrete will do the trick when laid in the appropriate dimensions on a code-compliant foundation. If the hearth is of a weighty material like slate, it must be installed on a concrete foundation that extends like a shelf out from the fireplace's foundation.

CHOOSING MATERIALS

Mantel—and fireplace—style is defined as much by the materials used to construct it as by the form that it takes. Some materials are integral to the construction of the fireplace, and others are applied once the masonry or wood-framed core of the fireplace and chimney is completed. Some mantels, for example, appear precisely built as if created by a machine, whereas others are folksier, crafted as one-of-a-kind sculpture.

There are many sources for mantels, the most direct being a home center, where you can select fireplace components out of a catalogue of traditional profiles. But don't be limited by what you see in the catalogue. There are also vintage or restored mantels for sale at flea markets or antique stores. Bring a list of your fireplace's dimensions and a pocket-size tape measure when you are hitting the salvage yards. Showrooms that carry stone also have stone and cast-stone mantels, and prefabricated concrete or plaster mantels are available.

Once your mantel is in place, you can select the appropriate materials to finish the surround. Using the correct terminology with a salesperson is helpful when selecting materials. The "head" is the part of the surround that runs horizontally along the top of the fireplace opening, just beneath the frieze and above the firebox. The "legs" or "slips" are the portions that run vertically along each side of the opening.

Brick

In the United States, brick has been used to build fireplaces since the 17th century. Most brick is reddish in color, but there is also gray, yellow, black, and brown brick. You can create different design effects by varying the colors and coursing patterns of the brick. Historically, the colors reflected the pigments of the local clay beds, but now you can find many varieties in most locales. Reds are the most organic and traditional bricks, and these are best suited for nearly all historically designed interiors. Standard-size brick as well as elongated and glazed versions lend themselves to more contemporary settings. It is also possible to find recycled antique brick that has a weathered patina. Bricks are now machine made so that they are identical, but occa-

The Art of Fire

Hearth: High or Low?

One basic decision in designing a fireplace is determining the height of the hearth off the floor. A hearth that sits on floor level is traditional and allows for a taller fireplace opening in a room with only a standard 8-ft. ceiling. When the fireplace is at floor level, the hearthstone can be set into the finished floor, which creates continuity and a more sophisticated look. Sometimes adding a thick hearthstone creates a situation where it is not perfectly flush with the surrounding floor. Adding a beveled wood strip around the edge is one way to prevent stubbed toes. Another is to make sure that the stone is thick enough to be noticed and avoided.

There are reasons to elevate a fireplace well above the level of the floor. A taller hearth may provide a bench and also brings the fire closer to your line of sight. In a room with a high ceiling, the fireplace opening often looks better proportioned if it sits higher up on the wall.

ABOVE: Corbelling, the placement of bricks to project outward, is employed to form a decorative element at the top of this fireplace.

RIGHT: Natural stones from pebbles to boulders are combined to form this sculptural fireplace. The shape of the firebox is unusually tall and narrow, nicely offsetting the heavy horizontal runs of stone.

FACING PAGE: Dressed stones look best when the mortar joint between them is very thin. Here, a skilled mason set the tightly jointed chimney stack around this prefabricated fireplace.

sionally clinkers, or irregular bricks, are produced. Historically these have been used for decorative effect in Arts and Crafts style homes, and are still used for new chimney and fireplace designs for a handcrafted look.

Natural and cut stone

Various sizes and shapes of stone are often used to face a concrete block–built fireplace and chimney, as much to conceal the block as to add additional masonry mass for long-lasting radiant heat. Natural stone, or fieldstone, is stone that has been

Fireside Lore

MODULAR BRICK

The idea of a standardized brick size comes from a 1625 English law that was modified to fit American preferences. Back then, bricks were slightly larger than today's nominal brick size of 9 in. long by 2⅔ in. high by 4 in. deep.

ABOVE: Rather than a miter joint at the corners, it is more typical to extend the head over the top of the legs so that it appears that the horizontal part is bearing on the vertical legs. Strong veining patterns in the stone help to disguise the joints.

RIGHT: A stone mantel with these proportions is built of smaller parts that fit together like a puzzle. Slight irregularities and veining are prized qualities that add to the material's sense of timelessness.

shaped very little by chisel or saw, and results in a rustic fireplace face. Some stone arrives at the job site dressed, which means that individual stones are shaped by chisels to create more uniformly flat facets. Dressed stones are called ashlar, and their squared-up faces and sides mean that they fit together more easily and the joints between them are thinner.

Slab stone is natural stone that is removed from the quarry in very large boulders and then sawed into large, thin pieces. The ¾-in. or 1¼-in.slabs of slate, granite, or limestone are adhered to the face of the substrate—the block or brick of the fireplace—by concealed clips and mortar. Some varieties are very colorful and heavily veined, whereas others, like some limestones, are more uniform in color and pattern and may contain minute fossils.

Slab stone presents a more uniform, continuous surface on the face of a surround than individual pieces of tile or brick. For example, in a high-ceilinged room an undersize fireplace opening will look less squat if the exposed surround is wider at the head than at the sides, and slab stone can be cut to virtually any dimension.

Molded stone and concrete

Soft stone such as marble and limestone has been carved since the days of the Greek temples. These stones are easy to work with and can be shaped and polished to a high sheen. Some mantels are quite elaborate and carved with intricate designs that incorporate scrollwork, human figures, or bas-relief sculpture. Others are more austere, with simple, elegant proportions, where the beauty lies in the stone's veining or unique coloration.

Cast stone has been a common building material since the beginning of the 20th century, used on the exterior of buildings for capstones, door and window lintels, and quoins. For fireplaces, molds are taken from one-of-a-kind antique mantels or created from new wooden versions and filled with a composite of fine aggregates and concrete. Multiple copies are cast, pigmented, and finished to look just like the real thing.

Concrete is a versatile material that can take many forms, colors, and textures. It can imitate tile, with small units grouted to appear like individual pieces. In most states, concrete is a less-expensive alternative to natural stone and can be poured into molds and assembled to look like marble or tile. Alternatively, you can celebrate its industrial aspects by pouring it into a wall-sized form for a monolithic mantel. Adding pigments is the perfect way to customize the color. You can polish concrete as smooth as glass, or create "wood grain" with certain formwork. Various objects, like seashells or glass beads, can be embedded in the concrete and polished smooth for a terrazzo finish.

Molds taken from antique carved mantels are recast in a very dense plaster. They are left white or faux painted to look like real stone.

TRON WE KRWI
VERSACE/AVEDON

have smooth, monolithic surfaces that can be hammered, bent, or rolled into a variety of patterns and shapes. Metals are noncombustible, but some will discolor or deform when exposed to high heat for long periods of time if their gauge is too thin. Some metals require polishing regularly to keep up their shine, whereas others develop a soft patina with age that some people prefer for its velvety surface.

Tile

Tile has long been used to decorate fireplaces and stoves, both for its heat resistance and the variety of shapes and colors available. Colonists imported the prized blue and white ceramic tile from Delft to

FACING PAGE: Poured concrete, stripped of its formwork, retains the imprint of the wooden form's grain, blending well with the surrounding timbers.

LEFT: This prefabricated lightweight concrete mantel was poured off-site and delivered ready for reassembly in place. This is a good alternative for modernizing an existing fireplace.

BELOW: A graphic composition of positive and negative spaces is made by combining narrow strips of wood around a flue shaft clad in knotty pine.

Wood

There is a natural inclination to touch wood, especially when it's crafted into a handsome mantelpiece. You can purchase traditional wood mantel designs and custom fit them to your own fireplace, or you can commission a made-to-order mantelpiece out of exotic woods. Wood mantelpieces come in many prefabricated styles, and there are also many antique wooden mantels available from salvage yards or antique stores.

Wood is lighter and more malleable than stone and lends itself to finer detail in carving and shaping. A wood mantelpiece will stand out if finished with natural stain and polished like fine furniture, or recede into the wall if painted to match the moldings and trim.

Metals

Historically, cast iron has been used in fireplaces in one way or another since the 17th century. Cast iron firebacks were originally formed by pouring molten iron into molds made from wooden forms that were pressed into damp sand. Today, cast iron is used for fireplace tools and inserts, but other types of metals are also finding their way into mantelpieces. Metals like stainless steel, copper, and bronze

ABOVE: A corner fireplace is a good location for a monumental copper hood spanning the distance from wall to wall. It's the focal point of the room.

RIGHT: The gothic arch of the fireplace opening is made more dramatic with a contrasting pattern of tile lining the inner face.

FACING PAGE: Tile need not be limited to the surround. A variety of glazed tiles are used here to distinguish the mantel, hearth, and surround, heightening the sense of craftsmanship and texture.

grace the slips of their fireplaces, and this tradition persists. Today you can find ceramic tile imported from around the world, plus glass, stone mosaic, and even metal tile.

Mosaic tile, whether it is stone, ceramic, or glass, comes glued to a 12-in. by 12-in. mesh or paper backing material to ease the installation process. You can cut the mesh into strips and interweave different colors, or you can pop out a few tiles in a random pattern and substitute them with another color tile.

With larger tile, a surround looks best with full tiles in the configuration. A full tile at the upper left and right corners of the head anchors the decorative pattern of the tile layout, with any cut tiles located within the surround. It is best, however, to design the surround and select tiles that won't have to be cut, or at least never use less than half of one tile in any part of the surround unless it is part of an overall pleasing pattern. A sliver of tile is difficult to cut, and will look like an error.

MANTELPIECE DESIGN

Once stoves replaced fireplaces for cooking and heating, fireplaces became sought-after architectural features and decorative accessories. The fireplace was referred to as "the domestic altar" in *The Woman's Book*, a compilation of housewifely advice, decorating tips, and social etiquette published in 1894. Fireplaces were opportunities for design flourishes, much like fancy stairways or ornamented doorways. An open fire was also a sign of wealth, as fuel and servants to tend to the hearth cost money. Mantels imported from Europe were status symbols for those who could afford to install them in their homes.

Built-in cabinetry

In the intervening 100 years, styles of fireplaces and mantelpieces have continued to evolve and grow. Paneling, elaborate overmantels, and entire walls of cabinetry that incorporate books, electronics, and display spaces are now part of the fireplace experience. These days, an evening sitting around the fire is almost a planned event, complete with special food and drink and company. In some arrangements, there is competition for attention between the fireplace and the television. Carefully designed cabinetry can balance the tension between the two focal points so that at different times of the day, or during different sorts of events, each can take center stage.

TELEVISON: CONFLICT OR COLLABORATION

Most of us can't discuss the location of a fireplace in a room today without considering the placement of that other focal point in our home, the television set. Do we place the furniture to face the television or the fireplace? The competition for attention between those two features has resulted in some compromises and some clever ways to accommodate both.

If the room is big enough, a fireplace can occupy one wall while the television occupies the wall at a right angle to it. Seating can mirror the right-angle arrangement, so that depending on which side of the coffee table you sit, you have a straight-on view of either the fire or the screen.

Flat-screen plasma televisions can be mounted above the fireplace, a space often reserved for a painting or mirror. That way, the sofas and chairs can face one direction.

Another solution is a retractable screen for a projection TV mounted above the fireplace. The screen can retract when not in use and doesn't compete with the fireplace. Older television sets with deep bodies can be recessed into niches next to or above the fireplace and, if desired, closed off when not in use.

It's best to conceive of the fireplace wall as a whole, with component parts of fireplace, cabinetry, and windows forming a single composition.

Cabinetry that shares the wall with your fireplace looks best when it is designed simultaneously with the mantelpiece. There are some basic guidelines. For example, when you're designing built-ins around your fireplace, first sketch out the wall with the fireplace and any windows or doors that share the space. Take inventory of the items that you want to display or store and make note of adjacent furnishings that face the cabinetry. This will help you to clarify the best spots for some items, such as televisions, audio speakers, and artwork.

Think about bookcases: Placed on either side of a fireplace, they complete the setting. Find a common horizontal line of cabinetry to link the bookcases with the mantelpiece to reinforce the continuity of the elements sharing the same wall.

Setting the height of the mantel is a design decision that depends on the height of the room relative to its width. This arrangement looks most balanced when the topmost shelf does not exactly bisect the wall. In a room with 8-ft. ceilings, try setting the mantel height at 5 ft., and in a room with 9-ft. ceilings, 5½ ft. or more is about right.

Keeping the Flames in Check

Stop in to any fireplace shop and you will be struck by the variety and quantity of accessories to keep the fire in the firebox where it belongs. Screens, andirons, and fenders have a long history of use, and glass doors were developed to preserve the heat as well as to protect.

ABOVE: Glass doors can close the firebox off from the room safely. They are not made of ordinary tempered glass; rather, they are a specialized ceramic safety glass that can withstand very high heat without cracking. Direct-vent gas fireplaces require that the glass doors remain shut, as the gas fire draws all of its combustion air through an exterior intake vent.

LEFT: Fenders corral rogue coals and embers fleeing from the grate and remain useful barriers today. They traditionally are used in conjunction with andirons and are most often made of polished brass.

BELOW LEFT: Andirons serve two purposes: to allow oxygen to reach and feed the fire and to prevent the logs from rolling out. Decorative andirons abound, and, like these with Hessian soldiers, should be selected to complement the mantelpiece and vintage of the home.

BELOW: Screens are either stationary, self-supporting on legs or curved bottoms, or retractable on a miniature curtain track mounted to the underside of the firebox's lintel that allows you to open it up to tend to the fire. When space for a cumbersome freestanding screen is at a premium, a hanging screen is your best option.

When decorating your mantel, consider that a grouping of similar objects is more effective than a parade of disparate elements. Here, the more the merrier, especially when reflected in the over-mantel's mirror.

Decorating your mantel

The mantel shelf is where we put our most prized possessions on view, like family photos and lumpy clay sculptures that your kids made. But your mantel is also a spot that should be redecorated now and then.

Selecting and arranging mantelpiece decorations is an art. Symmetrical arrangements are easy, as long as you have two of everything, but a balanced composition doesn't have to be rigidly symmetrical. Wintertime is the natural time to refresh your mantel, setting out holiday decorations and hanging greenery, but summertime is also a chance to display seashells or set a vase of fresh flowers on the mantel. Try clustering three or five tall candlesticks or vases of varying heights or materials at one end of a mantel and visually balancing them with a squat fishbowl at the other.

Don't overlook the firebox when it comes to mantelscaping. Fat candles set on the floor of the

LEFT: Your eye is naturally drawn to the fireplace in any room, even with no fire burning in it, so the mantel shelf becomes a prominent display area.

BELOW LEFT: The tapered brackets supporting the mantel shelf and the use of river rock as a natural fender at the hearth are examples of the Arts and Crafts sensibility used in a rustic setting.

BELOW RIGHT: Cabinetry incorporating electronics and a prefabricated fireplace employs careful alignment of seams and panels to break down the overall bulk of the piece.

Fireplace implements are a substantial investment but are essential tools for tending a fire and cleaning out the ash.

hearth or in one of the many candelabras offered just for this purpose are an easy way to light things up without laying an actual fire. In the warmer months, this is an especially nice way to brighten up the hearth.

Lighting your mantelpiece to show the artwork and objects on display to their full advantage can be accomplished with either a pair of sconces or a ceiling-mounted spotlight set to shine on the chimneybreast. Picture lights, which are discreet fixtures that mount directly on a painting's frame, are another alternative. All of these light fixtures should be wired with dimmer switches so that you can raise or lower the light level depending on whether you are having a rousing game of poker or a romantic evening in front of the fire.

Designing your own mantelpiece is an opportunity to create tangible memories. The inscription on this custom-designed mantel reads "*Ornamenta domus amici frequentantes,*" or "The ornaments of a house are the friends that visit."

The Art of Fire

Children and Pets

Children and pets are fascinated by the warmth and dancing flames of a fire, but they don't always comprehend the dangers. The safest way to prevent a tragedy is to take some simple precautions.

- **Never leave young children alone in a room with a burning fire.**
- **Purchase an expanding safety gate and completely surround your woodstove or fireplace, leaving at least 4 ft. of clear space on all sides.**
- **Hide the matches. Children can be tempted to start their own campfires.**
- **Use a fire screen to keep sparks or embers from reaching a basking pet's fur.**
- **Teach your children to respect the power of fire by instructing them in the proper way of tending to the flames and responsible disposal of embers and ashes.**
- **Keep children, especially toddlers, from coming in contact with glass doors, since they can cause serious burns in an instant.**

ABOVE: An assembly of candles both in and on the fireplace enlivens what is otherwise a darkened recess, and is easily ignited and extinguished.

FACING PAGE: Traditional fireplace brooms are short-handled affairs with the bristles tied into a round bundle, not spread out flat. They work quite efficiently, although you must wait for the ash to thoroughly cool before sweeping.

Tools of the trade

A poker, shovel, and broom—or sometimes a pair of tongs in place of the broom—are essential items for tending a fire. With pokers and tongs you can shift smoldering logs around to reignite the logs, and a shovel is essential for cleaning out accumulated ash.

Historically, on cold winter evenings farmers would make brooms to supplement their incomes. Early brooms were no more than bunches of twigs tied around a stick, and tended to fall apart quickly. Eventually, a variety of corn called *sorghum vulgere* was used as broom-making material because of its long tassels. We refer to this variety today as "broomcorn."

Fireside Lore

COLORFUL FLAMES

Gather dried pinecones and soak them overnight in a solution made with one gallon of water and one pound of dissolved Epsom salts. Remove the pinecones and let them dry. You can toss them a few at a time on the fire for a colorful rainbow effect on the flames.

“A stove will provide many hours of pleasure and heat.”

CHAPTER

4

Stoves

A FIREPLACE IS LIKE A FAMILY MEMBER, INTEGRATED INTO THE STRUCTURE IN THE HOME, WHEREAS A STOVE IS ALMOST LIKE A CREATURE THAT YOU'VE INVITED IN AND AGREED TO CARE FOR AND FEED. IN RETURN, A STOVE WILL GIVE YOU MANY HOURS OF PLEASURE—AND HEAT. THESE DAYS THERE ARE MYRIAD STOVE STYLES AND COLORS, FROM TRADITIONAL BLACK TO ENAMELED CAST IRON, STEEL, TILED, AND SOAPSTONE. ENAMELED STOVES COME IN A RAINBOW OF COLORS; RED IS THE flashiest, but blue, green, and brown are also available to match a variety of home styles. On the other hand, antique stoves are just as popular, as old-stove enthusiasts scour flea markets and estate sales to fill out their collections, and spend hours restoring old stoves the way some people restore old Chevys.

It's no small decision to install and maintain a woodstove. Even if it is not the primary heat source for your house, some care must be taken in selecting its type and size. Besides wood, of course, there are stoves that burn coal, oil, and biomass fuels—fuels made of organic waste products (see Chapter 5). This chapter will take you through the ins and outs of woodstoves.

There are logistics to take into account when considering whether or not to install a woodstove. Although a typical stove can easily fit through the average 3-ft.-wide front door, its weight is an issue. The average weight of a cast iron stove is anywhere from 200 lb. to 450 lb. Most homes constructed in the last century will have no problem sustaining that load, but in some cases the floor joists may need additional support to reduce the "bounce" that is inherent in any wood floor. If the floor is too springy, the masonry hearth under the stove can crack.

FACING PAGE: Part appliance, part companion, a woodstove is a good choice for a mudroom that sees lots of use in cold weather, particularly when there's room for a bench.

LEFT: A new cast iron stove must be seasoned like a new pan by building a series of small fires in it. Too big a fire too fast will crack and warp the cast iron.

The Art of Fire

Old Stove Clubs

The popularity of televised antique shows and Internet websites has spurred a new generation of collectors of unusual items. Enthusiasts and collectors of antique stoves can tap into these organizations' websites for products, publications, sources, and information:

- **www.antiquestoves.com**
- **www.theantiquestovexchng.com**
- **www.oldtymestoves.com**
- **www.goodtimestove.com**

Look for local dealers in your phone book or keep your eyes open at flea markets and yard sales. Locate an estate liquidator in the Yellow Pages® or the bargain newsletters. Stoves are heavy to move and don't have a lot of value to anyone but a real collector, so you might be offered a stove for free if you'll haul it away.

Decorative tile walls protect drywall and reflect the stove's heat back into the room. This European-style stove uses small pieces of wood to generate a hot, fast fire.

WHAT TO CONSIDER

Stoves must be set on a properly insulated noncombustible hearth, which resembles a small tile, stone, or brick patio inside your house. If the hearth is site-built, you will need to incorporate insulation—like cement board, fiberglass batt, or a product known as stove board—to keep the floor from scorching, as well as a noncombustible surface for ember protection.

A hearth's insulation value is determined by measuring how much heat it takes to raise a 1-in.-thick square feet of material 1°F. This measurement is designated the "K-value," and stove manufacturers list this in their literature. The lower the K-value for a material, the better it insulates. K-value is not an indication of noncombustibility, only a material's insulating quality. The noncombustibility aspect of the hearth lies in its finish—tile, brick, or stone. If you choose not to construct your own hearth, you can purchase premade UL-approved hearths for your stove.

Budget

Determining the cost of a stove involves comparing features and prices directly from manufacturers, installers, and websites. First, consider the initial purchase cost of the stove and its installation,

When a stove burns with its doors open, it operates just like a fireplace. While the efficiency of an airtight burn chamber is lost, the green doors offer a full view of the flames.

A centrally located stove and long stovepipe radiate plenty of heat in all directions in this open plan.

The burn chamber

The heart of a simple stove consists of one interior chamber where the fire is laid, accessible through a hinged door. Most stoves on the market today are a combination of cast iron and steel, which can withstand the intense heat of the fire. The heat radiates through the metal carapace, the stove's shell, and provides even, long-lasting heat. As the fire burns, the hot gases and smoke are exhausted through a stovepipe that extends from the back or top of the stove and through the chimney flue, which vents to the outdoors.

Some stoves have multiple chambers within the stove to create a longer path for the smoke and gas to travel, thereby releasing more heat. A series of baffles and dampers within more sophisticated stove models rely on this principle. The baffles force

A healthy stack of wood can fit neatly in the built-in space behind the stove, keeping the floor space free and clean and saving steps to the woodpile.

which can run anywhere from $1,000 to $12,000 or more, depending on the model that you choose and the mechanics of setting it up. Second, there are the fuel costs, which vary depending on where you live and the type of fuel you'll burn. Finally, factor in the cost of maintenance, including an annual cleaning and periodic replacements of parts. Any stove retailer should be able to give you a good idea of what these costs will be. It's important to consult more than one.

HOW A STOVE WORKS

When shopping for a stove it helps to know how a stove works and what optional features are available, and to understand that a stove is a bit more than just a fireplace-in-a-box. A well-designed woodstove is 50 percent to 75 percent efficient, and for home heating use can be expected to burn about a third of the amount of wood as a traditional fireplace. This is because the enclosed fire chamber creates the perfect environment for an efficient burn, one that uses nearly all the potential of the fuel in complete combustion. Less room air is lost up the flue than in a fireplace, which means that more heated air finds its way into the room. A stove's surface area also is a factor in its ability to radiate heat from all of its sides, especially if it is located in the middle of a room.

Anatomy of a Woodstove

The two types of woodstoves are catalytic and non-catalytic types. Catalytic stoves provide a more even heat, but require a little more finesse to operate than their non-catalytic counterparts. From the outside, they are virtually indistinguishable from one another.

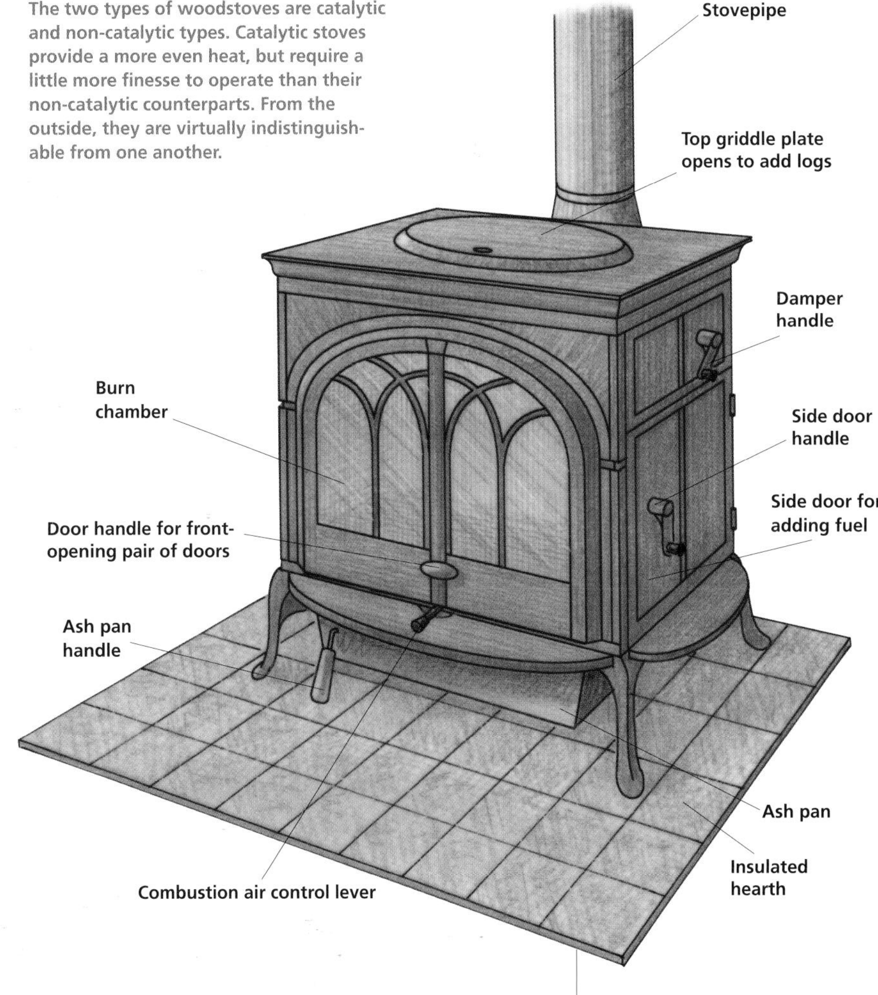

Fire Physics

For an optimum wood fire, there must be a moisture content of about 15 percent to 20 percent in the wood, enough oxygen for sufficient combustion and enough heat to get the process started. Burning kindling evaporates the water and resins in the wood at about 200°F and allows the logs to absorb the heat. As the temperature rises, volatile gases and tar vapor are released from the wood, a reaction called pyrolysis, and when the gases reach the flash point at a temperature of 480°F to 500°F, they will burst into flame.

The volatiles (the gases and tar vapor) burn off just above the surface of the wood, reaching a temperature of 1,100°F to 1,200°F and releasing about a third of the wood's potential energy. If the right amount of oxygen is not present, the temperature won't rise high enough and many of the volatile gases will be released as smoke.

The remaining material is charcoal and contains the other two-thirds of the wood's energy. The combustion of the charcoal takes place right at the surface of the charred wood and appears as an orange or white-hot glow that can reach temperatures of 1,300°F.

the volatile gases to pass over the top of the flames for a longer time, so that they completely combust.

Woodstoves control oxygen flow via a damper, an air-control device, and operable doors. This adds to the efficiency and capability of the stove to burn wood slowly and evenly or fast and hot. The damper is set in the open position as the stove is lit, and once the fire is underway the damper is closed to divert the smoke through the combustion zone, or firebox. The stove's air-control mechanism regulates the airflow into the firebox, controlling the rate of combustion.

Catalytic combustors

All new woodstoves on the market today must meet certain standard requirements to be listed and certified by the Environmental Protection Agency (EPA) for legal sale and use. There are two main categories of approved stoves: noncatalytic and catalytic. Each type has a different mechanism for reducing particulate emissions—the amount of smoke and soot it releases. Both types of stoves are designed to burn efficiently, reducing the amount of particulates released into the atmosphere by as much as 90 percent.

A catalytic combustor is a disc made of honeycombed glass or industrial ceramic and coated with a metal, such as platinum, which is the catalyst. It is installed across the opening to the exhaust vent so that as smoke passes through the honeycombs it reacts with the catalyst. The catalytic reaction lowers the ignition temperature of the gases (smoke) so that they are burned more completely. In noncatalytic stoves the stove's design must create an environment where the gases can reach the desired temperature for long enough to ignite the flue gases.

Stove maintenance

All the parts and pieces of a stove are designed together as one working system in order to function properly and provide a place for a clean, safe fire. Fortunately, parts and pieces can be exchanged for new components, so the life of a stove

ABOVE: This fireplace recess was designed to hold a stove. The supporting lintel is set high for dramatic effect and allows you to see more of the stovepipe.

FACING PAGE TOP: Keeping wood off of the floor means not only a cleaner look but also a cleaner stove.

FACING PAGE BOTTOM: A small stove can produce a surprising amount of heat to supplement a central-heating system. With a long stovepipe like this, there's the added benefit of the heat it radiates into the room.

On Fire

Catalytic Combustor

For a catalytic combustor to operate most effectively, it needs to hold a temperature of 600°F for at least 10 minutes. If a combustor is exposed directly to flames, it will be damaged, so a close eye on the burn is paramount. Most stoves equipped with these devices have a thermometer to gauge the temperature or a window to watch it. Catalytic combustors need to be maintained with periodic cleaning of the accumulated fly ash, creosote, and soot. They don't last forever, however, and need to be replaced periodically over the life of a stove.

MONOPOLY
MONOPOLY STAR WARS

EPA Regulations for Woodstoves

Woodstoves produce significant pollutants in the form of particulates and dangerous gases such as carbon monoxide. To reduce the impact of these emissions on people and the environment, the EPA developed certification requirements that govern woodstoves made after July 1, 1988. To comply with EPA standards, woodstoves and inserts sold today in the United States must release less than 4.1 grams per hour of particulates in the discharged gases if they are equipped with a catalytic combustor. If they don't have a combustor they may not release more than 7.5 grams per hour of particulates.

In addition, they must have a firebox volume under 20 cu. ft. and weigh less than 1,764 lb. The EPA posts a list of certified stoves on their website, www.epa.gov/woodstoves/basic.html, so you can easily check if your stove is compliant.

can be extended with good burning practices and maintenance.

The doors keep the stove airtight with a fireproof fiberglass rope gasket that should be periodically inspected for wear and replaced if necessary. The stovepipe will also corrode over time, but sections can be swapped out for new ones. The thimble, the collar around the stovepipe as it enters the chimney flue, may come loose and need to be reset. Finally, both steel and cast iron stoves will rust unless they are kept dry and clean and are periodically repainted with high-temperature paint to protect against rusting.

Stovepipe and chimney pipe

Stovepipe, also known as the chimney connector, connects the stove to an existing nearby fireplace's flue, in the case of a retrofitted installation, or to a new flue or chimney pipe. Chimney pipe differs

FACING PAGE: The masonry heat shield on the wall behind this stove absorbs the heat and will continue to radiate it back into the room even as the fire wanes.

FACING PAGE: Two 90-degree turns is about the limit to the number of twists a stovepipe should make. Too many slow down the flow of smoke, increasing the chance for creosote to collect in the flue.

TOP: This box stove's stovepipe connects to the chimney flue by way of a thimble at the wall, which protects the surrounding framing and acts like a gasket, creating an airtight seal.

BOTTOM: An oxygen-rich fire will burn faster and keep the exhaust gases moving quickly through the stove and chimney pipes even if the pipe is not completely straight.

from stovepipe, in that chimney pipe must be UL-approved Stainless Steel Class "A" Insulated Chimney material, whereas stovepipe is 24-gauge or 22-gauge metal tubing painted black.

Stovepipe is sold in sections of various diameters —the most common being 6 in. and 8 in.—and lengths in straight and bent sections. The sections are fastened with sheet metal screws and sealed with black furnace cement. The straightest configuration from the firebox to the chimney pipe will give you the best upward draft.

Stovepipe Configurations — You can extract even more heat from your stove if you extend the length of stovepipe within your home so that heat can radiate out of the surface of the pipe itself. However, too many twists and turns slow down the passage of the hot gases, cooling the smoke and creating the potential for creosote to form inside the chimney pipe.

Both single-wall stovepipe and double-wall stovepipe, which has an insulating air space between the outer and inner layers, are available.

The insulating space of a double-wall stovepipe keeps the smoke hotter as it vents, thus improving the draft, or draw. The tradeoff is that with a double-wall stovepipe less heat radiates into the room.

The thimble

Stovepipe should not penetrate a wall, ceiling, or floor without protection against fire. If the stovepipe passes through a stud wall to reach the chimney, a special device called a thimble must be used. A thimble is an insulated sleeve that will protect the surrounding materials. When installed there should be at least a 4-in. gap all the way around the thimble in which to stuff rock wool, a mineral-based insulation material.

ABOVE: A modern stove with a catalytic combustor is nearly half as efficient as a noncatalytic stove, but the air intake and temperature must be monitored carefully for optimum performance.

RIGHT: Antique stoves are not required to be listed by testing agencies, and don't come with warrantees and owner's manuals. Safe operation of these old-timers is a matter of experience.

If your stovepipe taps directly into an existing masonry chimney and ceramic flue, another type of thimble is required that fits into a hole made through the face of the chimney behind the new stove and joins the stovepipe to the flue, providing an airtight connection

FINDING THE RIGHT STOVE FOR YOUR SPACE

When shopping for a woodstove, there are a few things to keep in mind. You'll need to calculate the space, or volume, that your stove is to heat. (Cubic volume is measured by multiplying the length by the width by the height of the room.) Consider, too, if the stove is the sole source of heat for the space; if it is, you'll need a larger stove than one just for supplemental heat.

Also, consider its location. If the stove is situated in a corner, it will radiate heat in a different pattern than if it's in the middle of a room. Adjacent walls, large panes of glass, and the opening and shutting of nearby doors will all contribute to the movement of air through the "microclimate" created by the burning stove. A good rule of thumb is to estimate that you'll need 36 Btu per square feet for a room with an 8-ft. ceiling and 45 Btu per square feet for a room with a 10-ft. ceiling. Each stove on the market today is labeled with the number of Btu it can potentially release.

You should look at the product specifications for each stove to see if they meet your requirements. The specifications should include its average efficiency, the size of the logs it burns, the maximum floor area it can heat, its dimensions, and the range of its heat output.

Listed versus unlisted stoves

Stoves are either "listed" or "unlisted." Listed stoves are manufactured stoves that have been reviewed by testing laboratories such as UL or an inspection agency such as the EPA and have particular, measurable characteristics that meet or exceed government standards for safe use. Unlisted stoves are site-built custom stoves, those that are antique and so manufactured before this legislation, or those that do not need to comply, such as wood-burning masonry heaters.

CLEARANCES — The International Building Code (IBC) and National Fire Protection Agency (NFPA) restrictions dictate the clearances between a stove and stovepipe and any surrounding walls or windows. Unlisted stoves must stand a minimum of 36 in. and stovepipes a minimum of 18 in. away from any combustible materials, which this includes walls or ceilings covered in drywall. Wood or the paper facing on drywall can ignite at

A tempered, heat-resistant glass hearth plate is an unexpected high-tech touch in this traditional style room but matches the simple lines of the stove.

temperatures as low as 200°F if they are exposed to the heat over an extended period of time.

Listed stoves should be installed according to the manufacturer's recommendations. Some listed stoves can sit as close as 8 in. away from combustible materials if they are connected with double-wall stovepipe. The material that faces the nearby walls is also addressed by the codes, as are the range of materials and specs for a noncombustible hearth. Most hearths are brick, tile, or stone, but some are made of tempered glass.

To get the most heat, put a noncombustible masonry surface on the wall behind the stove. The masonry will soak up the heat and then release it over time, even after the fire has died down. This is a great design opportunity for a wall of tile or brick, textured fieldstone or concrete, or a single slab of honed granite or limestone. Decorative sheet metal, like stainless steel or copper, is a striking option, and will have the opposite effect. Instead of soaking up the heat it will reflect it back into the room as the fire is burning.

STOVE SAFETY

It's important to be aware of some basic safety concerns regarding the installation and use of stoves, particularly if you have small kids or pets. First, have your stove installed by an experienced and knowledgeable professional in accordance with the manufacturer's instructions. The following are a few other safety tips:

- Never use kerosene, gasoline, or any other liquid fire starter to get a fire going in the stove.
- Make sure there are no draperies, upholstered furniture, or rugs in the vicinity of the stove.
- Keep a fire extinguisher or bucket of sand nearby, but not behind the stove, because in case of an emergency the last place you'll want to reach is behind the stove.
- Do not burn anything other than kindling and well-seasoned wood or the approved pellet material in the stove. This is not the place to destroy old documents.
- A smoke detector should be located far enough away from the stove that the stove doesn't set it off under normal use.
- Check your stove often for wear, corrosion, or cracks. Check the thimble for loose sealant or loose stovepipe.
- Clean your stovepipe annually, and always when the creosote buildup is ⅛ in. thick or more.
- Do not empty the ashes until they are cool enough to touch with your hands (wait if there's any doubt about the temperature of the ashes) and never put them in a flammable container.

Installing a veneer of brick or stone on drywall isn't enough to protect the wall from scorching. Any kind of heat shield or wall protection must avoid too much heat transfer to combustible wood and drywall underneath. The wall will catch fire unless there is sufficient air circulation or insulation between it and the heat shield—an inch or so behind the masonry veneer will do. Sheet metal has good thermal conductivity so it disperses the heat quickly, but must also be mounted about an inch from the wall.

ABOVE: A masonry heat shield and insulated hearth like this faux stone arrangement is a deterrent for sparks and also protects the wood framing and floor from the intense heat.

RETROFITTING A FIREPLACE FOR A WOODSTOVE

By the mid-1800s, the cast iron stove replaced the open fireplace as a source for heat. Even now it makes practical sense to retrofit a smoky, inefficient, and drafty fireplace into a receptacle for a heat-producing, economical stove. The new stove sits on the existing hearth, and the stovepipe is connected to the chimney flue in one of three ways. If the stove is small enough to sit within the firebox the stovepipe can exit the stove out its top and go directly up through the fireplace's throat. If the stove sits in front of the fireplace there are two options: The stovepipe can go back into the firebox through the bricked-up fireplace opening or it can connect to the existing flue above the fireplace throat straight through the chimneybreast.

In some cases the existing ceramic flue may be damaged and so poses the threat of a chimney fire. Also, gases may escape into the house. In this case, the flue must be relined with metal for the new stove.

Fireplace inserts

A fireplace insert operates like a stove in that it consists of a fully enclosed firebox with an adjustable damper and an air-flow regulator to control the amount of oxygen reaching the burn chamber. The insert is an add-on device placed in the mouth of the fireplace opening. It has shields around the top and sides that fit tightly against the face of the existing surround. These make an air-tight seal that prevents any room air from being sucked into the burn chamber, so the oxygen needed to feed the flames is drawn from outdoors or under the floor. The face of the insert can be flush with the surround or can extend as much as 6 in. into the room.

LEFT: Blocking up an unused fireplace is an opportunity to display a decorative tile backdrop for a new woodstove, combining the features of both.

Insert units have doors, often glass, that prevent the room's heat from escaping up the chimney when there is no fire burning. Some also have fans that increase heat distribution, pushing more heated air into the room and less up the chimney.

Finding the Right Insert — You'll never see some of the working parts of a fireplace insert,

as they are located above the firebox and inside the chimney. In essence, an insert is a system of components that works together to give you a safe, efficient, enjoyable fire.

If you're shopping for an insert, you'll find single-wall and double-wall models. Single-wall models pull cool air from beneath the firebox and send it up in the space between the unit and the masonry wall of the fireplace, then send heated air out through ducted grills at the top of the unit into the room. Double-wall models, which are more common, safer, and more efficient, have an additional air space between the inside wall and the outside wall of the unit itself, which acts as insulation and creates a better environment for complete combustion.

Building code regulations require a mechanical connection through the fireplace's throat between the top of the insert unit and the lowest section of the flue. This connection, or metal sleeve, fastens the insert's exhaust pipe directly to the flue, eliminating any leaks and directing the smoke and hot gases up and out. Without this, there is a danger of smoke blowing back into the house, creosote buildup, and the potential for a chimney fire.

Most inserts require a new metal flue liner. The liner reduces the diameter and friction within the existing flue, and therefore increases the speed of the smoke and gases up and out of the chimney. Flue liners also solve any potential problems posed by old and cracked ceramic flues, which can be fire hazards. Because fireplace inserts burn more efficiently, they also burn hotter, and an old, neglected ceramic flue may not be able to take the heat.

With its doors closed, the fire in an insert burns more efficiently. A traditional open fireplace burns at between 20 percent and 50 percent efficiency, whereas manufacturers claim that an insert burns at as much as 80 percent, meaning that more heat is extracted from the wood fire and less warm air is lost up the chimney. Vents draw in air from beneath the floor or from the outside, which means that little air from the room is drawn in, reducing drafts and heat loss. Plus, adjustable air-flow regulators allow you to control the amount of air reaching the flames. Because inserts burn wood slowly and at high temperatures, they burn cleanly, reducing particulate emissions, or air pollution, to almost zero. This also means that less ash is created.

ABOVE: This stone fireplace wasn't adequate for heat, so a fireplace insert was installed. With its doors open it functions like a fireplace. With its doors shut it increases itsefficiency nicely.

LEFT: The firebox opening of this brick fireplace is fitted with a cast iron front, which radiates heat efficiently.

FACING PAGE: A picturesque yet inefficient fireplace becomes a safe niche for a woodstove. The stove exhausts straight up into the chimney, with a special fitting at the fireplace's damper.

STOVE STYLE

The granddaddy of all modern stoves is the plate stove, first brought to our shores by Dutch, Swedish, and German settlers in the first half of the

Quaint as it may be, an old brick fireplace might have a damaged flue. Installing an insert will require you to reline the chimney with a stainless steel flue so you can enjoy the fire again, safely.

the 18th century. Grooved cast iron plates were fitted together to form a firebox with an open back that was set against the back side of a brick or stone fireplace in the kitchen and vented through to the fireplace's chimney. The fire was laid through an access hole in the rear of the fireplace in the adjacent room. These stoves provided heat for the "stove room," but it was difficult to keep the fire burning as there was no way to introduce fresh air into the burn chamber. Plate stoves were the predecessors of the Franklin stove, or "Pennsylvania Fireplace," invented by Benjamin Franklin.

Box stoves

The design of the box stove dates back to the first part of the 19th century, and evolved from the plate stove. These were fairly modest and utilitarian appliances. The smaller sizes were found in homes, and the larger ones in churches and one-room schoolhouses. They have, predictably, a box shape and are simply decorated with cast iron designs. They are distinguished by a wide hearth plate that extends beyond the firebox. The hearth plate houses the damper mechanism and protects the floor from sparks and ash when the stove door is opened.

THE FRANKLIN STOVE

Benjamin Franklin's interest in solving the problem of smoky fireplaces, and a concern for the amount and expense of wood that a fireplace used in a season, prompted him to invent what we know as the Franklin stove, a cast iron firebox that was placed in front of the traditional fireplace opening. It stood on legs and consisted of a hearth for building a fire just under an overhanging cast iron plate. By using the principles of convection, smoke was directed down a channel behind the firebox that led under the floor of the hearth and then up through the chimney. In addition, fresh, cool air was admitted from the basement through a second chamber, heated, and permitted to radiate through louvers into the room. He called this contraption a "Pennsylvania Fireplace." Its design is the basis for what has evolved into the American woodstove.

Because it stood out from the wall, heat radiated out in all directions, and the cast iron body released heat even after the fire died down. His 1742 invention was widely received, and although the governor of Pennsylvania offered Franklin a patent, he declined it on principle: "That as we enjoy great Advantages from the Inventions of others, and this we should do freely and generously," as he wrote in his autobiography. Franklin-style stoves are still produced today, and antique versions are being restored to good use.

Cookstoves

The invention of the kitchen cookstove was the housewife's great liberation from the tedium and danger of cooking on an open hearth. Smaller fires and various chambers and burners meant that meals could be prepared more quickly and the heat regulated more easily. Cookstoves were black cast iron and later enameled steel. They are still useful in homes that don't have electricity or gas fuel. If you purchase an old cookstove, make sure that it is inspected and repaired by a professional.

Step stoves

A step stove, an early style of cookstove, has a unique stepped shape, with a fire chamber in the lower front compartment that heats the flat cooking surface above it. The upper portion is an oven that is also heated by the fire below.

The no-frills box stove has a Shaker sensibility to its design. The stovepipe's length is sufficiently long to radiate a great deal of heat into the room before it attaches to the chimney flue.

RIGHT: The kitchen was the warmest room in the house year-round when this step stove was used to cook three meals a day.

BOTTOM: The cast iron cookstove, much safer than cooking over an open flame, was attainable by middle-class households.

Parlor stoves

Cast iron parlor stoves evolved after the cookstove took the place of the open hearth in the kitchen and before the age of central heating. The main room in the house had its own stove, and this was a housewife's pride. Parlor stoves were affordable for the average household, and many antique versions survive. Some have translucent panels made of mica or isinglass, a natural mineral substance that can withstand high temperatures and, in thin sheets, is almost transparent. The more ornate stoves have nickel trim, cast iron designs, and stylish splayed legs.

Potbellied stoves and cylinder stoves

Potbellied stoves and cylinder stoves are specific styles of parlor stoves. The potbellied stove has a distinctive protruding belly, mushroom top, and guardrail at its "waist." It is the classic stove you picture when you think of the stoves that heated general stores, saloons, and railroad depots.

The Art of Fire

Furnished with a Stove

The mass production of inexpensive cast iron stoves during the Industrial Revolution of the 19th century saw many old fireplaces bricked up or hidden behind walls. In cities, stoves took up less room and weighed less than massive fireplaces. Although fireplaces were in an integral part of the house, stoves were more like appliances, and as consumer products they were advertised and upgraded.

With a cookstove you could more effectively regulate the heat than over an open fire, showcase your cooking skills, and use less wood or even use coal as a fuel. There was a decorative element to parlor stoves, with designs cast into the surface of the stove and eye-catching details like brass trim. Each principal room in a house had its own stove, and keeping them clean and well-maintained was important, as it was a matter of pride in one's housekeeping.

Part ornament, part heater, the parlor stove has a more vertical silhouette than the earlier box stoves and takes up less floor space when it's backed up against the closed-up fireplace.

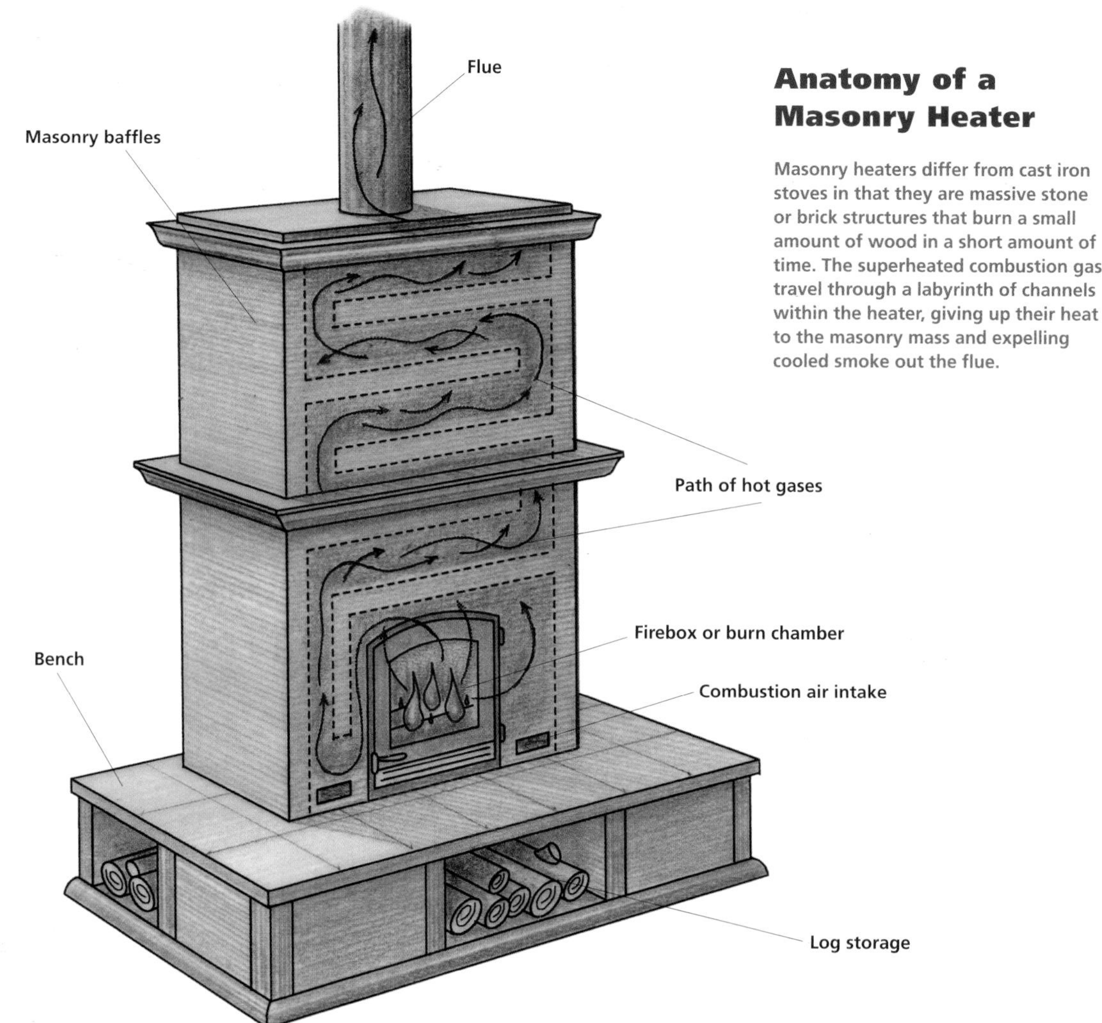

Anatomy of a Masonry Heater

Masonry heaters differ from cast iron stoves in that they are massive stone or brick structures that burn a small amount of wood in a short amount of time. The superheated combustion gases travel through a labyrinth of channels within the heater, giving up their heat to the masonry mass and expelling cooled smoke out the flue.

A potbellied stove has a characteristic mushroom top that increases the surface area for heating while it keeps a mug of coffee warm.

Cylinder stoves are thinner and more decorative, with a finial at the top and nickel trim and handles. Because they were so much more decorative and more expensive than potbellied stoves, cylinder stoves were most often used in people's homes or offices.

MASONRY HEATERS

"Masonry heater" is a rather bland term for what is called more colorfully a "Russian stove" or "Russian fireplace," the distinction being whether the fire is visible or hidden behind doors. Masonry heaters were used throughout Scandinavia, Russia, and Eastern Europe for centuries, and utilize the basic principle that stone and brick are excellent for heat storage, accumulating and then radiating the captured heat for hours. In European communities where the wood supply was limited, masonry heaters used only a fraction of the firewood that

This Russian fireplace looks organic, as if the house grew around it, but to achieve this look you'll need plenty of space to accommodate its large footprint.

a blazing hearth required. These days, in areas of the countryside that are "off the grid," the masonry heater is a good choice for heat.

In the enclosed firebox, cool combustion air is vented from the outdoors so the fire burns at a terrific heat, expelling equally heated gasses with very little particulate emissions. There is a masonry labyrinth within the flue so that the hot gasses produced by the fire run through a series of twists and turns before reaching the chimney flue, giving up their heat over the journey through the masonry mass.

More than a stove

Many masonry heaters integrate a bake oven, because the heat is high and even for long periods of time. Some have benches or platforms as part of their construction, which hearkens back to

The labyrinth of brick within this masonry heater extends under the lower portion to warm the soapstone bench, making it the best seat in the house on a chilly day.

early models of such heaters that were used as warm sleeping platforms long ago in rural Europe, Asia, and the American Southwest.

Modern masonry heaters are site-built from concrete, brick, or stone. Specialists holding a certificate from the Masonry Heater Association are experts in the intricate construction of these stoves. They must be masons, engineers, and artisans all at once to craft these well, as there is no tinkering with the insides once these stoves are completed.

Brick is a common facing material on masonry heaters. Besides storing and radiating heat well, brick is inexpensive and versatile enough to be laid in a multitude of patterns, arches, and curves. It can also be matched to the face of the chimney above.

Specialty concrete block is available with colorful glazed or textured, split-faced surfaces that lend a rustic look. Soapstone, admired for its smooth, blue-gray honed surface and its ability to retain and emit heat, is also a popular choice. It is quarried in slabs and presents a more monolithic surface on the face of a masonry heater than module brick, block, or tile. Tile, either glazed or unglazed, is a commonly chosen material as well.

Tiled stoves

Known alternately as German *kachelofe* or Swedish *kakelugna,* varieties of tiled stoves—a type of masonry heater—were imported by immigrants from northern and eastern European countries. First manufactured in the 17th century, these are freestanding, factory-made porcelain ceramic stoves covered with colorful ceramic tiles. Tiled stoves require just a small amount of firewood and provide a great deal of radiant heat. These stoves are lit in the morning and warm the room nicely for the bulk of the day. The tiles remain temperate to the touch, not burning hot.

Regardless of type or style, all stoves add to the character of a home and are a reflection of the homeowner's commitment to a more hands-on home heating system. Among the variety available,

On Fire

What Is a Cord of Wood?

A cord of wood is a standardized volume of split logs measuring 8 ft. long by 4 ft. wide by 4 ft. high. That should add up to 128 cu. ft. of fuel, but because there are air spaces between the stacked logs, the actual amount will be more like 80 cu. ft. to 90 cu. ft. of fuel. If you are sold a "face cord" of wood, that's a stack that is 8 ft. long by 4 ft. high and as wide as the length of one log. A "unit" is one-twenty-fourth of a cord of wood.

Logs are cut anywhere from 12 in. to 48 in. long. Make sure you know how long a log needs to be in order to fit into your fireplace or stove before you order the cordwood. ("Bucking" is the term used to describe cutting logs down for use in a particular fireplace or stove.)

Fireside Lore

Wood Poem

These hardwoods burn well and slowly,
Ash, Beech, Hawthorn, Oak, and Holly;
Softwoods flare up quick and fine,
Birch, Fir, Hazel, Larch, and Pine;
Elm and Willow you'll regret,
Chestnut green and Sycamore wet.

The tiled stoves of northern Europe were praised by Mark Twain in his travel writings. These decorative masonry heaters can heat a room at a comfortable, even temperature all day long from a small bundle of sticks.

HEAT

Heat from a fuel-burning device like a fireplace or stove is transferred from one substance to another in three ways, but all occur at the same time.

Radiation: The warmth from the sun that we feel on a sunny winter day is radiant heat. Radiant devices are low tech, transferring heat onto nearby objects or people directly. The radiant heat coming from any object depends on its temperature: The hotter the object, the bluer the radiant heat, and the cooler the object, the redder. In a fireplace, radiant heat from the fire is what gives the flames red, orange, andblue colors, indicating the different temperatures of the flames.

Convection: Convection is the transfer of heat by a liquid or gas. Above the flames, the hot smoke rises up through the chimney or stovepipe, drawing cool air from the room into the fire. Convective devices use a heat-transfer system to heat the air before redistributing it into the room. Some fireplaces and stoves have vents below that draw cool air, heat it, and release it through vents above the firebox.

Conduction: Conduction is the transfer of heat by a solid object. When the walls of the fireplace get hot, the molecules in the walls vibrate faster and cause their neighboring molecules to also vibrate faster, transferring the heat through the walls and to the rest of the house. The thickness and material of the fireplace walls helps to slow down the speed of the heat transfer so that the rest of the house doesn't get as hot as the fire.

from rustic to ultramodern, tiny burners to room-size masonry heaters, there is a stove for any application.

HEATING YOUR HOME WITH WOOD

In the early days, Americans relied on the bountiful forests to provide fuel for heating and cooking, but cutting trees and splitting logs was hard work even if the fuel was free, so more efficient fireplace designs and stoves were developed over the decades to get the most out of every cord of wood.

In homes without an oil or gas central-heating system, some homeowners still rely solely on wood-fueled heat in the cold months. However, heating with wood requires planning months in advance.

European-style stove designs now available in the U. S. are sophisticated modern appliances that utilize up-to-date technology to get the most heat from every log.

What to burn

Shrewd homeowners who fell their own trees or split their own wood learn to start early. Taking a tree down in the spring before the leaves are on it is easier and safer than doing it in the summer or fall because the tree weighs less, and once split, the logs have enough time to dry before they're needed for burning. If you are purchasing wood from a dealer, make sure you know when it was split, how long it has been drying, and the moisture content (the percentage of water left in the wood fibers). The ideal moisture content for optimum combustion is 15 percent to 20 percent.

All wood burns eventually, but some species are better suited and more readily available as fuel. The more dense, or harder, the wood, the better the burn. Deciduous trees like oak and maple are a better choice than pine or cedar because these hardwoods burn for a longer time than softwoods. Wood from fruit trees like apple, plum, or pear gives off a pleasant aroma. Some trees, like laburnum, are poisonous, meaning the smoke is toxic, and others, like poplar, emit an acrid smoke.

On Fire

Wood's Heat Potential

Each type of wood has a certain amount of potential heat measured in Btu per pound, depending on the moisture content of the wood. Resinous species of wood produce 8,600 Btu to 9,700 Btu per lb., and nonresinous woods 8,000 Btu to 8,500 Btu per lb.

In general, the average amount of Btu per lb. is 8,600. Denser species like ash have more potential Btu than lighter wood like poplar. Because wood is sold by volume—by the cord—it's important to know what species you are buying. Remember that hardwoods (deciduous trees that lose their leaves in the fall) possess twice as much heat potential in a cord of wood as softwoods (coniferous trees that retain their leaves or needles all year).

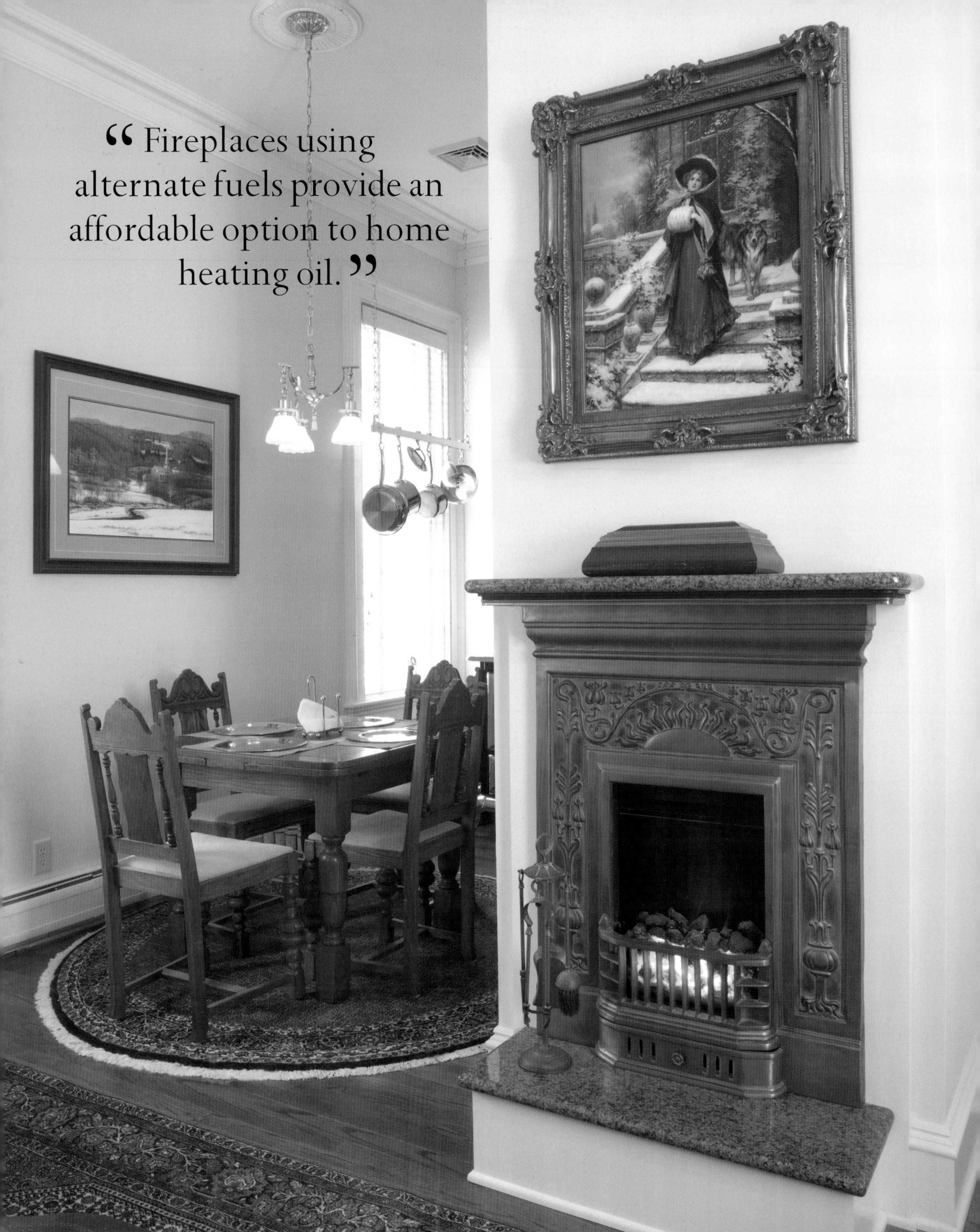

"Fireplaces using alternate fuels provide an affordable option to home heating oil."

CHAPTER

5

Alternatives to Wood

IMAGINE CONJURING UP A CRACKLING FIRE AT THE PUSH OF A BUTTON AND THEN EXTINGUISHING IT INSTANTLY FROM ACROSS THE ROOM. OR PICTURE AN AFFORDABLE ALTERNATIVE TO THE INCREASINGLY EXPENSIVE HOME HEATING OIL TO KEEP YOUR HOUSE COMFORTABLE ON A CHILLY DAY. YOU CAN ACHIEVE BOTH THESE DREAMS BY INSTALLING A STOVE OR FIREPLACE THAT BURNS A VARIETY OF FUELS OTHER THAN WOOD. WOODBURNING STOVES AND FIREPLACES, ALTHOUGH CERTAINLY TRADITIONAL, AROMATIC, AND PICTURESQUE, ARE NOT FOR EVERYONE. THERE ARE THOSE FOR WHOM A WOOD FIRE IS NOT FEASIBLE or desirable, especially if you live in a high rise or in a small apartment. Other folks may find their new home already sports a non-woodburning stove or fireplace. And still others may find that a woodstove or fireplace doesn't provide a convenient source of reliable heat.

The biggest distinction between woodburning and alternative-fuel stoves and fireplaces is the delivery system of the fuel. Wood has to be hand fed, as needed, and relies on someone keeping a watchful eye on the state of the fire. The alternate fuels discussed in this chapter are delivered to the burn chamber automatically according to a steady flow of gas or an electric mechanical feed system, and can be left largely unattended.

"Fuel-burning appliance" is industry terminology that refers to manufactured fireplaces and stoves. It's no surprise that their popularity is increasing. From 1998 to 2004 the quantity of alternative-fuel-burning appliances in the United States grew from 1.6 million to almost 2.4 million, whereas the quantity of conventional woodburning appliances—prefabricated fireplaces, inserts, and stoves—sold during the same period declined from

FACING PAGE: Gas appliances are inexpensive to install and don't always need a chimney for venting. They can be tailored to match a room's décor with a custom-designed mantelpiece and hearth.

LEFT: Gas fireplaces are not limited to make-believe logs. Sculptural metal forms are decorative even when there is no fire burning.

two-thirds of a million to less than half a million.

Manufacturers have worked hard to imitate the sight and sound of a wood fire. In many cases you may not even be able to tell the difference between an authentic wood fire and one of the alternatives.

FUEL OPTIONS

Depending on your fireplace or stove, you can choose between a number of organic and fossil fuels. Some organic fuels, like wood pellets, corn, or other biomass fuels, require a specialized type of stove, whereas fossil fuels such as coal, oil, or gas can be used in fireplaces or stoves that have been adapted for this use. Mostly, the appliances that burn these alternative fuels strive to imitate the flickering flames of a traditional fire within a fireplace or stove but with the convenience of an on-off switch or the rapid quenching of the flames when it is time to shut it down.

Organic fuels

Organic fuels are those from renewable sources like trees or plants. Besides the most obvious organic fuel, wood, you can burn wood fiber products—sawdust, shavings, and the like—that are compressed into small pellets or crafted into artificial logs. Discarded corn, nutshells, and fruit pits are other options for organic fuel, as well as "bio-diesel" fuels made from 80 percent vegetable oils. EPA certification requirements since the 1980s have contributed to the efficiency of all organic-fuel stoves and fireplaces, and as a result particle emissions have decreased as the efficiency of these appliances has increased.

Fossil fuels

Fossil fuels come from inorganic, nonrenewable resources, like coal mines, oil wells, or natural gas deposits, to provide us with coal, heating oil, propane, and natural gas. There is a limited global supply of fossil fuels, so the efficiency of the appliance and the fluctuating costs of the fuel are important considerations.

Although the development of coal and oil stoves preceded gas-burning appliances in the marketplace, most of the stoves and fireplaces

Fireside Lore

TELEVISED YULE LOG

The televised Yule log, a continuous film loop showing the flickering flames of a cheery fire accompanied by seasonal music, was created in 1966 by a New York City television station general manager, Fred Thrower, as a gift to fireplace-less apartment dwellers on Christmas. The original loop was only 17 seconds long, and the current Yule log's seven-minute loop is broadcast for about four hours without any commercial interruption.

FACING PAGE: The ease of installation and affordability of gas appliances has reintroduced fireplaces to traditional spots in the home, like kitchens, where they can be turned on with a switch.

BELOW: Artificial logs made of compressed fibers and waxes are a practical solution for a quick-burning fire on a romantic evening for two.

On Fire

Coal Stoves

In the mid-19th century, as wood sources were becoming less accessible, coal-burning stoves, also known as "baseburners," became the predominant heating source, especially in urban areas. Today, coal stoves are used primarily for heat, but you can still find decorative coal-burning stoves in many homes. If you are fortunate to live near active coal mines—in eastern Pennsylvania, for example—you'll find that you can obtain coal inexpensively. Many manufacturers still offer stoves that can be used for both wood and coal. Anthracite coal is the highest grade of coal and is regarded as smokeless and clean. Bituminous coal is softer and produces more soot and smoke. Nevertheless, coal, like oil, is a fossil fuel, and both produce significant pollutants, such as carbon monoxide.

RIGHT: Gas fireplaces don't require a conventional chimney, so this unusual setup permits the fire to be seen from three sides and the "mantel" to be used as a display surface.

BELOW: Gas fireplaces lend themselves to sleek and modern mantels and hearths unencumbered by kindling or fireplace tools.

purchased these days are fueled by gas, either natural or propane. Natural gas is measured in therms, whereas propane, or LP (liquefied petroleum) gas, is measured in gallons. One therm and one gallon each contain about 100,000 Btu of heat value.

GAS-BURNING APPLIANCES

Propane- or natural-gas-burning fireplaces and stoves, like their wood-fired equivalents, can be used to provide heat and a homey atmosphere. Prefabricated gas fireplaces are very popular, as they are simple to install and relatively clean burning, releasing only combustion gases with no visible particulates into the air. In regions of the country where new woodstoves or fireplaces are prohibited, such as in some of the western states, gas appliances are very common.

Most gas-burning fireplaces and stoves rely on piped-in natural gas provided by the local gas company. If natural gas is not available through the local utility company, some manufactured stoves and fireplaces can be converted to burn propane instead. You can contract with a local supplier to deliver large canisters of propane that sit on or are buried in the ground. Your local zoning and safety codes may require propane tanks to be stored securely away from driveways or other potentially hazardous spots.

A key benefit to gas appliances is the minimal maintenance they require. There is little soot and no ash to contend with, though an annual safety check by a certified chimney sweep to inspect the chimney and vents is recommended. In addition, your stove or fireplace should be professionally serviced every couple of years to keep it in top working order.

Gas fireplaces

Gas fireplaces are built in exactly the same manner as traditional masonry fireplaces but are outfitted with gas jets concealed by a log set, or synthetic logs made of fireproof material that are formed to look exactly like burning logs. When in use, the damper must be open. Some manufacturers block open the damper permanently for safety. To restrict air loss, glass doors on the face of the fireplace should be kept closed when there is no fire burning.

More typically, however, gas fireplaces are manufactured models installed the same way as a fireplace insert or prefab. These are lightweight steel fireboxes that are set within a wood-framed box and maintain a clearance of 1 in. to 2 in. between the fireplace unit and any combustibles surrounding it.

Prefabricated gas fireplaces don't need a deep hearth in front of the firebox like a masonry fireplace hearth extension. One reason is that there are no hot embers, so there's less of a fire hazard. The current edition of the International Building Code (2003) requires only that the hearth extension be installed in accordance with the manufacturer's listing of the fireplace and that the hearth be "readily distinguishable" from the surrounding floor area—for example, tile or stone contrasting with a wood or carpeted floor. But omitting a broad hearth is a dead giveaway if you are trying to simulate an actual wood fireplace. Some folks even purchase a poker, bellows, and other fireplace tools to complete the look.

Prefab gas fireplaces are generally intended for the convenience and pleasure of the flame, but some have the added benefit of being "heater-rated" and can be used for heating a room. When choosing a prefab fireplace, consider the size of your room and whether you need an actual heat supply or just ambient, supplemental heat.

In a twist on the usual arrangement, this gas fireplace is mounted at eye level above a recess. Its unusual square proportions and wide frame suggest a kinetic sculpture.

On Fire

Carbon Monoxide

Leave the installation of a gas stove or fireplace to the experts, but put a carbon monoxide detector in your home yourself. Carbon monoxide, one of the products of combustion, is odorless, colorless, and deadly. The Hearth, Patio & Barbeque Association recommends the use of a carbon monoxide detector as well as a smoke detector whenever a gas-burning fireplace or stove is installed, and also an annual checkup by a certified chimney sweep.

The TULIP
Anna Pavord

Gas fireplace inserts have either a pilot light or an electronic igniter. Electronic ignition is more efficient because you don't need to keep a pilot light burning all the time, but if the power goes out you won't be able to start the fire. A remote control start is another feature of an electronic ignition.

Gas Log Sets — The illusion of a natural fire would not be complete without crackling logs, so manufacturers have developed imitation logs that mimic the look of an actual wood fire. These fireplace logs are made of a refractory material such as concrete or ceramic fiber and can be purchased in collections of three or four for the homeowner to artfully arrange in the firebox of a traditional masonry fireplace. Granulated vermiculite, a naturally occurring fireproof mineral that looks a lot like kitty litter, is liberally sprinkled on the floor of the firebox to simulate a bed of ash. Makers of these gas log sets pride themselves in the "faux bois" look of their products, and you can choose from a wide variety of "species" to get just the right look.

Gas log sets are not intended to provide heat; they are more for the ambience of a wood fire. One of the criticisms of early model gas fireplaces is that the flame was too blue—more like a Bunsen burner than a cheery blaze. Manufacturers have resolved

ABOVE: The long-handled copper bed warmer propped up alongside this mantel is decorative. In fact, the gas fireplace doesn't require any tools or accessories.

LEFT: The gas fireplace is well integrated into the rustic scheme of this room, especially clad in brick and topped with a chunky wooden mantelshelf.

FACING PAGE: Gas fireplaces have no need for deep hearths to protect the floor or carpeting against flying sparks.

FACING PAGE: This unusual two-sided gas fireplace uses a miniature landscape of rocks to conceal the gas jets. The rocks can be shifted or replaced altogether as desired.

BELOW: In regions of the country where firewood is scarce, stone is a natural substitute for log sets, echoing the desert environment.

this problem so that the flames now mimic a real wood fire with yellow flames and "embers." Unless they are manually lit with an extra-long fireplace match, gas log sets need electricity to ignite them, so if you propose to use log sets, plan for the gas piping and the electrical service.

Not everyone wants to pretend they have wood logs burning in the fireplace. There are other ways to furnish a firebox to conceal the gas jets and provide a backdrop for the fire. Stones, cast geometric forms, cast pinecones, and other unusual items have found their way to the gas fireplace, and these alternatives are gaining in popularity.

Fireside Lore

MERCAPTAN

Natural gas and propane are naturally colorless and odorless. Mercaptan, or methanethiol, is the additive that gives gas fuel that rotten egg smell. After a disastrous explosion in 1937, the U. S. government required that mercaptan be added to gas and propane to aid in the detection of gas leaks.

Gas stoves

Gas stoves are also similar in look to their woodburning counterparts, but because they burn fuel at an even rate their ability to provide consistent heat is useful when you need to heat just a specific zone or space, like a separate family room. You might select a gas stove over a woodstove if you don't have easy access to firewood or if you prefer the convenience of an instant and evenly burning fire.

The selection of available gas stove styles runs the gamut from traditional to contemporary, and most are almost indistinguishable from their woodburning counterparts.

Gas stoves are sized by the number of Btu they burn per hour. Most give an approximate amount of square footage that can be heated and are grouped into three basic categories: small, medium, and large. A small stove that can heat up to 500 sq. ft. might burn from 7,000 Btu

1000 on 42nd Street
GUESS WHO

ABOVE: Both the gas-burning stove and its long stovepipe emit enough heat to adequately warm this space. A thermostat and continuous supply of gas keep it at an even, comfortable temperature.

RIGHT: The narrow stainless steel stovepipe vents the combustion gases upward via natural draft. The glass wall and see-through firebox mean that the fire is visible from outdoors as well.

to 11,500 Btu per hour, whereas a large stove intended to heat a space as big as 2,000 sq. ft. may have the capacity to burn from 20,000 Btu to 40,000 Btu per hour. Many models offer high and low burn settings as well as thermostatic controls, so the amount of heat is adjustable for comfort.

Stove manufacturers should also provide the overall efficiency of each model so that you can judge what the actual potential heat output is by multiplying the given input Btu by the percentage of efficiency. Many factors affect this rating, depending on the cubic footage and configuration of your home, environmental conditions like outside temperature, and the amount of glazing and insulated walls around the stove.

Gas stoves can be located according to the same guidelines that apply to any fuel-burning appliance in your home, and they require the same safety features and accessories. Gas stoves need to sit on a fireproof hearth pad, which can be masonry, tile, or even glass. They must follow the same precautions regarding proximity to combustible materials as woodburning stoves as well as all building code regulations.

Venting

There are three ways to vent a gas stove or fireplace. The first is natural draft, the conventional route that relies on a vertical flue and chimney to vent the hot gases and combustion products to the exterior. A double-wall "B" label metal flue is required for this, and may be hidden within a wood-framed shaft that runs up through the interior of the house or up along an outside wall. Woodburning stoves and fireplaces must use this standard venting arrangement.

A second venting option for gas appliances is a "direct vent," which means that there is no vertical flue. Instead, the hot gases and combustion products depart the firebox straight out the back or

No need to settle for a traditional-looking model; contemporary gas stoves patterned on European styles are suitable for a modern interior.

side through a fitting that acts as a sleeve through the wood-framed wall behind. All that is visible from the exterior is a metal box mounted on the face of the house. From the interior the appliance looks exactly like any prefabricated fireplace or freestanding stove. Direct-vent fireplaces and stoves must be located at the perimeter of the house. They operate with outside combustion air only, so the glass doors must always remain shut during operation to seal it off from the inside air supply. This allows them to radiate heat into the house without consuming any warmed room air.

Vent-free gas fireplaces burn so efficiently that they eliminate the need for any venting at all. However, they release water vapor and combustion products back into the room and rely on the room air to supply oxygen. In today's tightly built homes

Fireside Lore

Biomass and Biodiesel Fuels

Although biomass and biodiesel fuels come from organic waste products, the two can't be used interchangeably. Biomass fuels are solid fuels, such as wood pellets, which are used for fuel in stoves or furnaces. Biodiesel fuels are liquid fuels, such as corn oil, that are pressed from freshly harvested produce or recycled from industrial sources—like fry vats—for use in vehicles in place of gasoline.

This direct-vent gas fireplace is located on an outside wall and doesn't require a chimney. The glass panel must remain shut while the fire is burning, so that all combustion air enters the firebox from the outside.

LEFT: A conventional fireplace can be retrofitted for a pellet stove insert, converting a decorative feature into a working source of dependable, even heat.

RIGHT: Compressed-sawdust pellets are loaded into a hopper, then they're augered by the stove directly into the burn pot.

they can be a health hazard. Many states have outlawed the use of any vent-free or unvented appliances, particularly in bedrooms, as they are potentially dangerous due to the levels of carbon monoxide they produce. They also emit high levels of moisture into the house that can overhumidify the home and create health concerns like mold and mildew.

PELLET STOVES

Pellet stoves have only been around since the mid-1980s, when they were invented by Dr. Jerry Whitfield, an aeronautical engineer at Boeing® Aircraft. They were developed on the heels of the energy crisis of the 1970s as a way to use organic waste products—sawdust, for example—as economic fuel.

A better and more accurate term for those waste products would be "biomass fuel," which refers to organic byproducts from plant-based renewable energy sources, such as wood fibers, corn, straw, hulled wheat, nutshells, fruit pits, and other agricultural waste.

Pellet stoves are designed to look similar to conventional wood- or gas-burning stoves or fireplace inserts, but they have a unique fuel-supply

Anatomy of a Pellet Stove

Pellet stoves are increasing in popularity for supplemental heat as well as for the primary heat source in many homes.

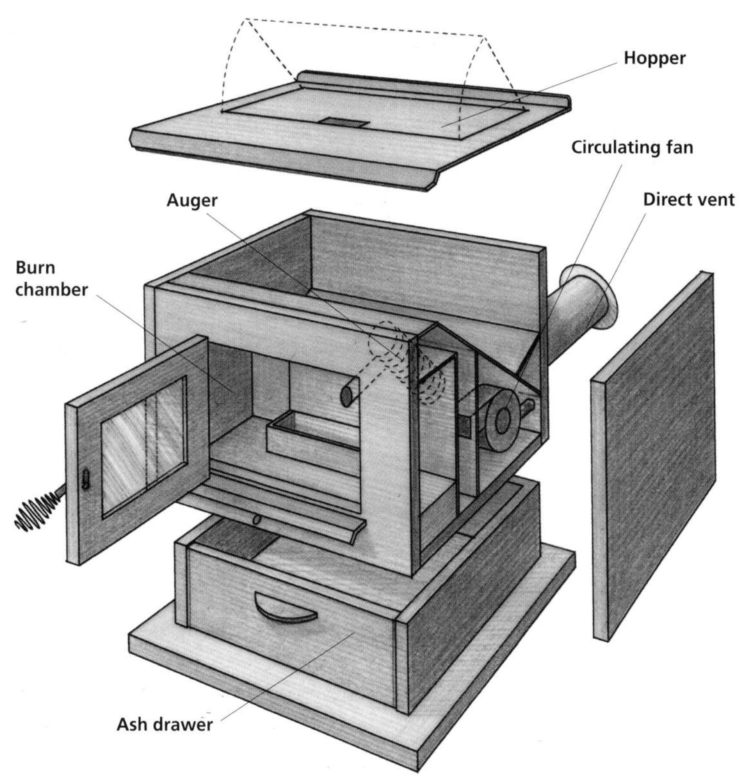

Pellet stoves require a noncombustible hearth and must be placed far enough away from any surrounding walls to comply with the manufacturer's installation instructions for safety.

feature so that the stove burns at a consistent rate. A glass window permits a view of the flames, and some models offer the use of simulated log sets to complete the impression of a wood fire. There are different sizes and capacities of pellet stoves, and their integral thermostats control the heat efficiently.

To operate, the fuel is manually loaded into a hopper, usually at the top of the stove. A hopper full of pellets can deliver enough heat to last 24 hours or more. An electrically powered auger system (like a big corkscrew) delivers the pellets, a few at a time, into the burn pot, where they are consumed. The rate that the fuel is dropped determines the heat output of the stove. In case of a power outage, some pellet stoves can be hooked up to a battery backup system to keep the auger moving and the stove alight. Clinkers, which are deposits that are created from the ash when it is heated and cooled repeatedly, and ash must be periodically cleaned from the burner and ash pan.

Over 600,000 homes rely on pellet fuel for heat, and the number is growing. The recently enacted Federal Energy Policy Act (July 2005) is an initiative that, once funded, will encourage more use of renewable energy appliances—like pellet stoves—by offering a rebate to consumers who use them. Our current reliance on fossil fuels may spark more homeowners to investigate this option, even if it is for a single room in the house.

Pellet stoves are exempt from EPA requirements for emissions yet exceed standards for all solid-fuel-burning appliances. They are touted to have efficiency ratings of 75 percent to 85 percent better than gas fireplaces or stoves. Because they burn so efficiently, less creosote builds up in the flue and thus they require less cleaning than a conventional wood stove.

Venting

Pellet stoves and fireplace inserts are vented in the same manner as gas-burning appliances. They can rely on natural venting up through a flue and chimney or they can be installed as direct-vent stoves. A conventional masonry fireplace can also be retrofitted for a pellet stove or insert, but the existing flue must be evaluated before assuming that it is usable for a pellet stove or insert. A pellet stove's stainless-steel flue is narrower in diameter than a conventional flue for a woodstove (only about 3 in. or 4 in. in diameter).

Pellet fuel

Each wood pellet is a uniform-size cylinder, about 1 in. long and the diameter of a pencil eraser. Natural resins hold the compressed sawdust together, and the pellets are packaged in 20-lb. or 40-lb. bags. Pellets are sold by the ton, and a ton of pellets is roughly equivalent to 1½ cords of wood. Two or 3 tons of pellets a year is sufficient to heat most homes, although much depends on climate and the size of the home. Because the cost of pellet fuel, like other fuels, varies by region, you can compare costs for where you live with a handy interactive chart located on the Pellet Heat Institute's website: (www.pelletheat.org).

On Fire

Wood Pellets

There are two grades of wood pellet fuel available: standard and premium. Standard may contain up to 3 percent and premium up to 1 percent inorganic ash content. Standard-grade pellets have more tree bark or nut hulls in their makeup, which creates more ash when burning. Premium pellets are made from more homogenous sawdust ingredients and produce less ash as a result. Most pellet stoves on the market can burn either grade, but check with the manufacturer's recommendations before using either fuel.

The most inexpensive fuels are those that are sold locally. In farming regions it makes economic and environmental sense to burn corn that can't be sold or consumed.

Corn stoves make good use of corn that's been rejected for animals and people.

CORN STOVES

The same technology developed for wood-pellet stoves is also used for dry-shelled corn-burning stoves. Many homes in farm country rely on corn-burning stoves for secondary or even primary heat. There is a great amount of corn that is not fit for

ABOVE: This electric fire unit needs only the depth of a stud wall for its installation. It can go in any room and is a good option for places where a fuel-burning fireplace can't be installed.

RIGHT: This electric stove imitates a coal grate and emits a glow like the embers of a bedded-down coal fire without the smoke, soot, or ashes.

FACING PAGE: A perforated gas line creates a linear fire in this new take on a conventional fireplace. It is reflected in the plate glass, doubling the effect.

human or animal consumption, whether damaged by rain or vermin. In the past, silos full of this rejected corn would be discarded, but this stove technology allows it to be put to use as an energy-efficient and renewable fuel source—especially if you consider that it takes only about four months to grow a crop of corn.

A bushel of corn, or about 56 lb., is enough for about a day's worth of heat for a 2,400-sq.-ft. home. With a corn stove, the average home will burn anywhere from 85 to 150 bushels of corn per heating season, depending on the climate and whether the stove is the primary or secondary heat source. Corn stoves are direct vent, which means they don't need an extensive flue and chimney system; the stove just needs to sit against an outside wall. Similar to pellet stoves, the electrically powered auger that feeds the corn into the combustion chamber will stop if the power goes out, so many homes rely on an emergency generator.

RIGHT: Forget the notion of authenticity and instead substitute a modern interpretation of nature. Steel logs in this contemporary home float between the hearth and the fireplace hood.

FACING PAGE: These extremely realistic logs are designed to "burn" inside a fireplace with the vent open but don't emit any soot or smoke.

ELECTRIC FIREPLACES

Sometimes the only solution to getting the look of a fireplace without actually installing anything that burns fuel of any sort is to use an electric fireplace. These have come a long way from the unreal fires used as stage scenery or department store window dressing. Most electric fireplaces rely on a gentle blower and fabric "flames" to imitate a wood fire with the clever use of glowing lights, though some also mimic coal fires with burning embers.

Gentle electric heat distributed by a fan to take the chill off a room is a manufacturer's option in most models, or you can just turn on the electric fireplace for the simple visual pleasure of dancing flames. Because nothing is actually burning, there are no fumes or any need for a flue or chimney or any sort of venting at all, just access to 110 volt or 240 volt current and a wall. Remote-control operation is another feature that makes electric fireplaces easy to use. In a bedroom you can "extinguish the flames" more easily than you can set your alarm clock.

EMERGING TECHNOLOGIES

Manufacturers continue to come up with unique ways to deliver fire into our homes safely, attractively, and affordably. If you consider fireplaces and stoves as "hardware" and the fuel that each burns as its "software," you can be sure that there is new software being developed for many applications. Manufacturers are developing new uses for waste products that would otherwise go to landfill and designing new products that allow us to install fireplaces in unexpected places.

Ersatz logs

Ersatz logs are made of compressed sawdust mixed with petroleum wax. Mostly you pick these up at the supermarket on a whim, to be set aflame with a match as your dinner guests ring the doorbell. Some have seeds incorporated into the log that pop when they burn, simulating the sound of a real wood fire. You can purchase these logs in various sizes to fit your fireplace and you can select versions that burn for different lengths of time.

Gas Detector Safety

You should always install a gas detector at the same time as you install any gas stove, fireplace, or insert. If it signals a leak, or if you detect a gas odor, immediately take the following steps:

1. **Send everyone else, including pets, out of the house to a designated safe location.**
2. **Do not switch on any electrical devices in the house—no light fixtures, televisions, or computers—and do not use your home telephone.**
3. **Close the gas taps and the gas meter valve.**
4. **Open windows to let in fresh air and leave the house.**
5. **Using your cell phone or a neighbor's telephone, call 911 or the gas company's hotline.**
6. **Don't reenter your house until the gas company has declared it safe.**

Recently, as a response to new clean-air regulations, manufacturers have come up with versions of these firelogs that are more ecologically pure, that do not have any binding agents that pollute when burned. These additive-free firelogs can be safely used for cooking in a barbecue because they are made exclusively out of hardwood and burn cleanly at a high temperature.

Gels and beyond

Sterno®, which is often used to warm food at a smorgasbord or buffet, is also available for use in specialized flueless "fireplaces"—wall-mounted mantels with shallow fireboxes lined with noncombustible materials. Cans of specially formulated sterno are placed behind artificial logs and ignited to replicate a wood fire. The mixture of isopropyl alcohol, water, salt, and a jelling agent also has an additive that causes it to snap, crackle, and pop, emitting only sound, carbon dioxide, and water vapor.

Another similar product called Flameco® pours into a special hinged holder that has artificial logs that fold back on top. These sit inside a prefab or conventional masonry fireplace and provide the same effect. Burning a scented candle that imitates the scent of pine or other favorite fireside aromas can enhance both of these gel products.

“Adding an outdoor fire place allows you to extend your living space even in cold weather.”

CHAPTER

6

Outdoor Fire Places

WHO CAN RESIST SPENDING AN EVENING SITTING OUTDOORS UNDER THE STARS WITH A ROARING FIRE NEARBY AND THE SCENT OF WOODSMOKE FILLING THE AIR? ADDING FIRELIGHT IN AN OUTDOOR FIRE PLACE BRINGS THE COMFORT AND NOSTALGIA OF A FIRE TO YOUR OUTDOOR LIVING SPACE YEAR-ROUND. WHETHER IT'S A STONE FIREPLACE SET ON A COVERED PORCH, A STYLISH FIRE PIT, OR A SIMPLE CAMPFIRE, A FIRE PLACE WILL EXTEND YOUR LIVING SPACE, ALLOW YOU TO ENJOY THE OUTDOORS EVEN IN COLDER WEATHER, AND CREATE GREAT AMBIENCE. YOU'LL EVEN BE ABLE TO ROAST MARSHMALLOWS while you soak in the night sky, and enjoy hot cider in the late afternoon. Add some furniture and accessories, and you will have created an outdoor room to use for entertaining family and friends or for quiet contemplation.

FACING PAGE: No matter the season, an outdoor hearth cheers and warms. Its appeal is universal, tapping in to our collective memory of gathering at the fire.

LEFT: The firelight illuminates this terrace. Small light fixtures mounted on the trellis above cast a romantic glow while adding brighter light for eating or playing games at the table.

THE FIRE OUTSIDE

Before you light your first match out of doors, take stock of the rules. Not all towns welcome wood fires outdoors, so it is important to check with the local fire marshal or building inspector before investing in or using any outdoor fire appliance.

Locate your fire safely away from overhanging tree limbs, roof eaves, and power lines. Even if the branches are 20 ft. up, the fire's hot combustion gases will singe and damage the tree and any creature on it. Unless the fire is contained in a fireplace, take care when putting one near a building. If it's windy, save the fire for another day.

Show consideration to your neighbors. Do not place your fire place close to your property line and be aware of which way the wind generally blows so your smoke doesn't blow into a neighbor's window or yard. An outdoor fire in any configuration is a

RIGHT: The weight of the stone has to be calculated carefully when sizing the supporting steel angles over the fireplace opening, especially on a two-sided fireplace.

LEFT: A comfortable seating area near the fireplace encourages guests to sit and enjoy the view. In an outdoor room the possibilities for accessorizing with furniture are practically endless.

The Art of Fire

Chimineas

A small portable stove, a chiminea adds style as well as heat to an outdoor room. Traditionally used for cooking and keeping warm inside small adobe dwellings in Mexico, chimineas were originally made of fired clay and had a bulb-shaped firebox with a short, narrow chimney on top. Similar versions with their distinctive bulbous shape are widely available today, as are more modern cast iron or cast aluminum shapes and models. They are typically supported on a tripod to sit several inches above the floor or patio.

Both clay and metal chimineas must be gradually broken in by building small fires that season the inner surfaces so that they are less likely to crack. Start by laying a 3-in.- to 4-in.-deep layer of sand or clean kitty litter at the bottom of the bowl, and place two bricks parallel to each other a few inches apart to create a grate on which to lay the logs.

To care for your chiminea through the winter, keep water from collecting at the bottom and freezing, which can crack the ceramic or damage the metal. If the chiminea is set outdoors on the lawn or a terrace, frost heaves can dislodge the base and topple it. So, although it is cumbersome, it's best to store your chiminea in a garage when not in use to protect it from the elements.

Decorative ceramic tile doesn't have to be limited to indoor fireplaces. These tiles add a bright spot of color to the smooth, clean surface of the stuccoed wall.

gathering spot for parties, so be aware of its proximity to those who aren't invited—they may not appreciate hearing campfire songs late in the evening.

OUTDOOR FIREPLACES

A fireplace set outside is just as inviting as a campfire or fire pit, but whereas a fire pit set within an outdoor room is like a piece of furniture, an outdoor fireplace architecturally defines the boundaries of outdoor living. Mostly this is due to its size and the height of its chimney, but also because we are conditioned to expect a fireplace to coexist with a building as its background. You'll find outdoor fireplaces incorporated into the side of a house, embedded in a garden wall, or freestanding, marking the boundary

Fireside Lore

CAMPFIRE COOKING

Early man discovered the benefits of ringing his fire with stones. The stones contained the hot ash and absorbed the heat from the flames, staying warm long after the fire died down. We've since learned that you can roast chestnuts, corn, or potatoes in the ash and enjoy a hot, tasty meal alfresco.

Bill's
Pizza

For pizza connoisseurs there is nothing better than a pizza oven built into an open hearth. Although the firebox opening is smaller than the typical fireplace, diners can still see plenty of flames while they eat.

Indoor/Outdoor Fireplaces

For greatest efficiency and least expensive construction, a fireplace within the house should be located within the perimeter walls, optimally at its core. However, there are design opportunities (and houses) that beg to differ. If your patio or covered veranda is adjacent to an interior room that's slated to have a fireplace, the same chimneystack can encase a second, outdoor-facing fireplace. Remember, though, that in all cases each fireplace requires its own flue, so an outdoor fireplace in this configuration must be planned and built from the beginning.

If you're adding an outdoor fireplace against an existing wall, you'll need either a new masonry chimneystack or a new wood chimney housing a prefabricated fireplace. Some manufacturers offer prefabs that are intended for outdoor use. Either way, it will require a new solid concrete foundation to be built alongside the existing fireplace.

FACING PAGE: It appears that the corner of the roof is supported on the chimney, but that is not permitted by code, so separate structural columns are encased within the cylinder to hold the roof.

between terrace and lawn. Some outdoor fireplaces are part of a larger configuration that includes a grill or other cooking appliances so that the beauty of the fire can be enjoyed while dining.

You might expect all outdoor fireplaces to be of a rustic stone design, reminiscent of picnic areas at state parks and campgrounds, but in fact outdoor fireplaces incorporate all sorts of styles and materials. You may choose to tie the style of your fireplace to that of the house, matching materials and detailing, or depart altogether into a fireplace that looks as if it grew out of the landscape. Metal, concrete, cast stone, and natural stone work equally well on outdoor and indoor fireplaces. Adding decorative ceramic tile or polished granite touches around the fireplace opening can dress it up to make it more formal or to personalize it. Outdoor fireplace accessories can also range from a pointed stick to a set of matching wrought iron tools.

Beneath the roof

Whatever you prefer to call it—veranda, porch, or covered patio—a fireplace in a covered outdoor living space is a delightful addition. Having a roof overhead means that you can still sit around the fire on a rainy day, and in the winter you won't

ABOVE AND RIGHT: This outdoor room is situated in the protected void between two portions of the cottage. Guests and residents meet at the fireplace for an evening drink before retiring to their separate wings at the end of the day. The fireplace anchors the courtyard and provides privacy from the street.

have to shovel the terrace in order to warm up during breaks between snowball fights. You can furnish this outdoor space much like an indoor one, with seating, tables, and lighting, and arrange those furnishings so that they face the fireplace.

If the fireplace is at the far end of your outdoor living space rather than backing the house's exterior wall, you should be able to see and enjoy the flames from inside the house. Not only does this draw your attention to the view out the windows but you will also be able to keep an eye on the fire from inside. Remember, however, that no fire should be left unattended, so make sure that someone responsible is keeping tabs on and enjoying the blaze outdoors.

Below the sky

Once the fireplace is released from the shelter of a roof it can venture farther out into the scenery. The elements of fire, air, water, and earth are a natural palette for creating a harmonious living space that is attuned to the landscape. To suggest the defining edges of an outdoor room, you can add an overhead trellis or arbor to create the illusion of a ceiling, and brick, concrete, or stone pavers to demarcate the floor. This "room" has boundless windows, so a fireplace introduces a solid focal point to enjoy when not gazing far afield.

In some backyards the fireplace is a part of a larger landscaping scheme, with a pool, barbecue, or long garden wall dividing one area of your back garden from another. There are advantages to incorporating a fireplace into a wall—the wall dampens the wind, making the adjacent terrace or yard pleasantly habitable on a cool sunny day, and provides privacy from nearby neighbors or the street. This sort of arrangement looks most coherent when the fireplace is made of similar materials as the wall, so there is continuity to the design.

A freestanding fireplace has benefits as well. By orienting it so that you can take in the view over its "shoulder," you'll have dual focal points, one foreground and one background, doubling the pleasure of sitting outside no matter the time of day. When a freestanding fireplace is set out into the landscape farther than 10 ft. from a building, the height of the chimney no longer has to conform to the building code requirement that it extend 2 ft. above the nearest portion of the house. However, you may decide to extend the height for aesthetic and performance reasons. A stumpy chimney will not draw well, and a smoky fireplace is not enjoyable.

Indoor versus outdoor fireplace

Although they look similar to one another, there are some tangible differences between an indoor and an outdoor fireplace. The biggest is that an outdoor fireplace has no need for a damper, as there is no concern about heat loss when it's not in use. The throat at the bottom of the chimney flue remains open to the firebox all the time. This simplifies its manner of construction, although you might find more rain and snow make their way down the chimney. A correctly constructed outdoor fireplace should therefore have a slightly outward-sloping hearth to assist water runoff.

Outdoor masonry fireplaces tend to be more substantial in size and their fireboxes proportionally larger than their counterparts that you would typically use inside your house. There is something about the limitless sky ceiling and wide horizons that would dwarf a puny firebox out of doors.

Outdoor fireplaces often have the firebox opening raised up 1½ ft. or so above the level of the surrounding floor. This is strictly a design decision and allows a better view of the flames, bringing them up toward eye level. If the fireplace is on a stone or

An outdoor fireplace paired with a pool will warm swimmers between laps and offer a soothing view from the spa. It also provides a degree of privacy fromnearby windows.

The Art of Fire

Luminaria

Sometimes all the fire you need is in one small flame. Conventional nighttime outdoor lighting is often harsh, more suited for a runway than a moonlit terrace. Gas lights have the benefit of being adjustable, so you can temper their intensity, and the glass shroud keeps the wind from extinguishing them with a gust. You might find a single fixture is enough, or you might prefer to ring your patio with several, igniting them all with a single switch.

brick terrace, you won't need a hearth extension, but you may want one anyway so you have a ledge where you can put your feet or rest a mug of hot cider. Don't forget to plan for storage of logs and kindling and other accessories. And get a screen to shield shooting sparks and to cut down on the wind blowing into the fireplace on a blustery day.

Unlike the many options for indoor fireplaces, outdoor fireplaces are typically built of masonry to withstand the elements. They may either have a solid core, like concrete block, clad with more stone or other weather-resistant materials (tile, stucco, brick, or metal), or be built out of individual field stones, stacked and mortared in place. Some manufacturers are beginning to offer prefabricated gas- and wood-burning models suitable for outdoor use, although you are more apt to see these used in the warmer climates of the South. Due to their continuous exposure to the elements, outdoor fireplaces rarely have a wooden mantelpiece.

Although chimney caps won't keep out animal intruders because there is always access to the chimney from below, caps are still useful as spark arresters on windy days.

Buying versus building

There's no question that outdoor fireplaces are a growing trend. With that growth has come an increasing number of manufacturers that offer stylish prefabricated metal or masonry fireplaces designed for outside use. From 2002 to 2005 sales of prefabricated outdoor fireplaces alone grew to more than 600,000 a year. This figure doesn't include the number of custom-built fireplaces crafted by masons, so the actual quantity is much higher.

For occasional use, consider a freestanding portable metal fireplace suitable for the outdoors. These smaller-size models can be stowed away between gatherings. They are generally less expensive than custom-built fireplaces, and manufacturers offer models to suit almost everyone. The most substantial of these are cast iron or cast aluminum alloy, but there are other styles made from copper or zinc-coated steel. One of the benefits of freestanding fireplaces is that if you change addresses the fireplace can move with you.

Some people prefer a beefier and more permanent cast-stone or custom-built masonry fireplace. The sturdiness and organic nature of the stone cladding make these fireplaces easier to integrate aesthetically into the nearby landscape. Precast fireplaces are attractive, but you are limited to what is currently on the market. There are sources for outdoor fireplace components that stack up like blocks and that you can finish in the field with any

FACING PAGE: Massive stones at the jambs, hearth, and lintel frame this rustic fireplace. It is set into the crook of the stone wall, creating an intimate corner for before-dinner drinks.

LEFT: A long-burning fire will heat the deep hearth extension so it can become a bench to warm chilly athletes enjoying winter sports.

BELOW: The outdoor side of this Rumford-style indoor/outdoor fireplace has the same stone patterning that's on the interior face, creating a cohesive, massive chimneystack.

PORTABLE OUTDOOR FIREPLACES

If you need a quick fix of fire for your terrace, you can purchase any of a number of models of freestanding fire bowls, fire pits, chimineas, or outdoor fireplaces for sale at home centers and at garden, fireplace, and patio shops. Some freestanding models are designed exclusively for providing heat, whereas others are designed for the pure pleasure of viewing the flames. Some models include a grill for cooking or a spark-arrester screen for added safety. To be truly portable, these need to be lightweight, so metal versions—copper, aluminum, and steel—fit the bill.

You must set any of these portable units on level ground and away from any combustible materials, including the side of the house. Do not place anything with an open flame on a covered porch, but an open trellis or pergola should allow the smoke to rise freely. Some products are touted to be safe for use on combustible surfaces, but use common sense when placing a fire pit or fire bowl on a wooden deck. At the very least, shield the flooring with one of the many protective mats that are on the market. Even better, never put any fuel-burning appliance on a wooden deck (including a grill), because metal appliances can transfer heat, scorching the wood. They should be put under cover when not in use. Never use water to quench the flames or you will run the risk of cracking the metal.

The surfaces of any of these portable devices become extremely hot, and so even if the fire seems to have burned out, keep children, pets, and your hands away for at least an hour after you see the last smoldering embers.

RIGHT: If you haven't used your outdoor fireplace in some time, clear the chimney of any animal nests and even birds, like chimney swifts, who like to make their homes in chimneys.

BELOW: Climbing vines embrace this stuccoed fireplace.

cladding that you desire. But just as for indoor fireplaces, there is no single product or method that is right for every backyard or every region of the country. If you want a fireplace that fits just right into your outdoor room or if your space has special considerations, you may want to have the fireplace custom built.

Working with the weather

Unfortunately, we can't control the weather, but if there is a choice of several locations it's a good idea to orient the fireplace opening to face the direction of the oncoming prevailing wind. This will help feed oxygen to the fire and direct most of the smoke up and out of the chimney, instead of toward you and your guests.

There is no magic formula for building an outdoor chimney that will never smoke, but there are things you can do to lessen downdrafts and encourage a clean-burning fire. The height of the chimney, wind, atmospheric pressure, and nearby trees and buildings will all affect the chimney's draw. Gusts of wind create turbulence that can force smoke back through the chimney or blow it down off the top of the flue. Either way, it can be unpleasant and unhealthy to be buffeted by smoke. Benjamin Franklin suggested the use of a wind vane at the chimney top to help prevent downdraft. A taller chimney draws better than a shorter one, and a decorative chimney pot can add some needed height while injecting some individuality into your fireplace.

The effects of freezing temperatures on the lifespan of outdoor fireplaces can't be minimized. Some outdoor fireplaces are built of block with a stone veneer, but others are constructed from stacked stones bonded with mortar. Fieldstone is a good choice; it's a dense, hard stone and can withstand large fluctuations in temperature. But when rain (or melted snow) seeps into any cracks within each stone or in the joints between the stones and freezes there, it will expand, potentially cracking or shifting the stones. Building a roaring fire in a cold fireplace may also cause cracks to form from the sudden shift in temperature, so build up the fire slowly, allowing the chimney to warm up over time. The solution is to select stones that are best suited for this use, like fieldstone or dressed granite blocks, and that can withstand harsh weather. Yearly maintenance, like repointing the mortar and brushing out the interior of the flue with a stiff brush, will extend the life of your outdoor fireplace.

Installation basics

Stone is heavy. Just as a firm foundation to support the massive tonnage is required inside the walls of your house for a masonry fireplace, the same is true outdoors. Site-built masonry fireplaces, inside or out, need a code-compliant concrete foundation to safely support them. This means excavating the earth to the frost line to lay a firm footing that won't heave in the winter. The depth will vary depending on where you live, so consult your local building official. Once the footings are in place, masonry foundation walls go up to support a broad concrete slab for the fireplace to sit upon. The fireplace's weight, therefore, is solely supported on a stable concrete foundation and not directly on the surface of the ground.

ABOVE: This bottle-shaped fireplace is an outgrowth of the terrace wall. Because it faces the stone terrace there is no need for a distinct hearth extension, which means you can get even closer to the flames.

LEFT: A tall chimney will improve the draw, especially when there are nearby trees and homes that affect the surrounding air movement.

Even though they are lightweight compared to solid stone versions, prefabricated cast stone fireplaces can weigh 2 tons or more and require firm foundations as well. These cast stone fireplaces will crack stone and brick terraces if pavers are merely set in stone dust rather than mortared onto a concrete slab that can withstand the weight of the fireplace. A prefabricated fireplace that's installed incorrectly can also be damaged over the winter if not properly mounted on a concrete foundation. Frost heaves can shift and potentially crack the heavy fireplace if it is placed directly on the ground.

Gas-fired outdoor fireplaces are powered by natural gas piped in from the house or from a nearby propane gas tank. Either way, you can enjoy them year-round just like a wood-burning fireplace. However, if there is an off-season for your outdoor gas fireplace, be sure that the gas is shut off from its

RIGHT: This fire-breathing, smoke-spewing fireplace is an attraction even when there is no fire on the hearth.

BELOW: This raised hearth and fireplace surround are tiled to match the nearby swimming pool surround. Specialized tile that can withstand a wide difference in temperatures without cracking is available.

FACING PAGE: The mason preselected the individual stones, sketched their arrangement, and directed the installation. The largest were lifted with a crane and mortared in place.

source and the remaining gas in the pipe is left to burn out—much like putting a gas grill away after use.

However you create your outdoor fireplace, it reinforces our primal connection to our shared ancestral fireside, providing a beacon of light that protects, warms, and provides nourishment to our hearts and stomachs.

FIRE PITS

"Fire pit" means different things to different people. To some, a fire pit is a big campfire built within a shallow hollow and intended as a place to cook food for several hours. For others, a fire pit is a location for a religious or ceremonial purpose, part of the rituals of many ancient and modern cultures worldwide, demonstrating the magical properties of fire and its connection to nature, purification, and rebirth. Today's definition of a fire pit leans more to the secular than the sacred, unless, of course, you consider toasting marshmallows a ritual act.

The benefit of a fire pit is that it illuminates as well as warms. It is possible to adjust the intensity of the flames on a gas-fueled fire, so you can create the look you prefer.

In today's parlance, fire pits are high-tech versions of campfires—chimneyless, open-sided fireproof containers that can be custom-designed permanent fixtures costing thousands of dollars or off-the-shelf purchases for under $100. There are metal, concrete, and masonry versions, both factory produced and hand built. Many fire pits are designed to be decorative outdoor centerpieces, although some do come with metal racks for outdoor grilling and screened covers for added safety.

Fire pits can be enjoyed year-round, so the surrounding seating area should accommodate both commodious lounging areas for a summer evening and a place to pull up a bench close to the fire in cooler weather. Like outdoor spas, swimming pools, and stone terraces, a fire pit is an increasingly popular outdoor fixture that is a pleasure to enjoy throughout the seasons and one that boosts property values, especially when built into the landscaping.

Fireside Lore

BALE FIRE

Celtic Druids celebrated the annual holiday of Beltane by preparing a bale fire, a ritual purification bonfire on the eve of May Day. On this eve all hearth fires were extinguished and a new communal bale fire was ignited to inaugurate the season of rebirth, fertility, and growth.

ABOVE: Indoors or out, the sight and sensation of a warm blaze on the grate is the best welcome home sign there is.

LEFT: A fixed fire pit alongside a house requires special planning so that it is safe. Check your local regulations before installing a fire pit next to the house; and you may want to work with a professional who can help you create the safest area possible.

Pairing fire and water is a dramatic juxtaposition. Here, the fire pit fits into the flagstone and fieldstone patio, and the ringing wall doubles as a seat near the flames.

What's burning?

Whether custom made or factory produced, you can find fire pits that burn either wood or gas. Burning logs within a stone, metal, or concrete fire pit is similar to burning wood in a campfire, although the fire pit may come equipped with more accessories, like a grate or a set of andirons. You will need to take precautions to contain the flames if the fire is big or if the day is breezy by placing a fire screen over the fire to shield any sparks or runaway embers.

The convenience of gas makes fire pits that burn either natural gas or liquid propane a good choice for instant on-off use. For custom-designed installations, you can purchase components, like gas rings in various diameters, to create a one-of-a-kind fire pit for your terrace or garden, but this is a project to be completed by experienced professionals. It could take a team of gas fitters, masons, and welders to complete the installation.

In well-designed fire pits the gas fittings are concealed within a gas log set or stones, or tucked behind other shapes made of refractory material to complete the authentic look (be sure to camouflage the propane tank, too, or you'll be giving the secret away). If your gas fire pit is installed out in the open, cover it when it's not in use to protect it from rain and snow, which can flood the pit and damage the gas lines. Be sure to purchase a model that you can light with an electronic pilot light rather than a match so you don't risk singing your sleeve.

Safety first

No matter what fuel you choose, fire pits will generate a lot of heat. Fire pits set into masonry will heat up the stone to some degree, but the density of the stone supplies some natural insulation and stone is a slow conductor of heat. Lightweight portable metal models, sometimes called fire bowls, lack the natural insulation of masonry, and are very good conductors of heat, so their surfaces heat up very quickly. Be cautious even when the flames have been extinguished, because the metal surfaces will stay hot long after the fire is out. Wood-burning models have that woodsy scent that we love, but because you can shut them off quickly, gas-fueled fire pits are a safer alternative.

CAMPFIRES

Most of us have an early memory of sitting around a campfire, perhaps roasting hot dogs at the beach or warming our toes after an afternoon of skating on Uncle Bob's pond. Campfires are low tech by definition: A ring of stones placed on the earth, surrounding blazing logs, is as basic a fire place as there is. You might choose to have a designated campfire spot in your garden, or if your property is large enough, you may move it to a fresh place from year to year so that the grass has a chance to grow back.

LEFT: When a larger fireplace would block a great view, a fire pit is the answer. Grouped with a slatted bench, this angular fire pit creates an inviting spot to enjoy the view from this hillside perch.

The optimum spot for a permanent campfire is well away from the house and surrounded by a gravel or stone patio. Ringing it with benches will make it a destination on a balmy evening.

By tucking the campfire into the natural depression of this rock ledge situated just below the crest of the hill, it is less affected by prevailing winds.

Fireside Lore

SMOKEY THE BEAR

In 1937, President Franklin Roosevelt initiated a poster campaign alerting people to the danger of forest fires with the enduring slogan, "Remember—only YOU can prevent forest fires!" In 1950, the Forest Service adopted the mascot "Smokey," after an orphaned baby black bear found clinging to a scorched tree after the Capitan Gap wild fire.

Building a campfire

Begin by digging out a shallow depression in the dirt about 4 ft. in diameter, removing any grass or plant material. Edge the perimeter of the bowl with stones as large as baking potatoes or bigger. Stack logs to form a tepee or lay them in log-cabin fashion, overlapping their ends, to form a triangle or square. If you are lucky enough to be building at the beach, you can gather driftwood to burn, otherwise use ordinary well-seasoned cordwood. You can use fallen branches, but they must be dry and free from rot or you will end up with a smoky fire that won't stay lit. Smaller dry sticks and leaves make good kindling to tuck under the logs.

Before you light the fire, make sure you have a hose or a bucket of sand or water nearby and take note of the wind direction. You may want to position the fire so that the smoke blows away from your seating area, and so any potential sparks won't land on anything combustible. A campfire can quickly become a bonfire if you feed it too much wood too quickly, and can get out of control. Never leave a campfire burning unattended; even if the flames have died down, a gust of wind is all it takes to revive the blaze. Extinguish the fire thoroughly with water or sand until the ash is cool enough to run your fingers through.

LEFT: A nighttime campfire casts a welcome glow and keeps the dark at bay. Digging a shallow pit and surrounding it with rocks is the safest way to enjoy the firelight.

On Fire

The Right Wood

In general, the same rules apply for choosing wood for an outdoor fire as for an indoor fire. Burn only seasoned hardwood. You might want to consider piñon. Its wonderful pine scent not only smells great, but it also wards off mosquitoes. Other woods with aromatic smoke, such as apple, also make great choices for an outdoor fire on a summer evening. Never burn chemically treated wood, trash, or material that produces toxic or hazardous fumes.

Glossary

AIR-CIRCULATING FIREPLACE
A fireplace that draws in cool room air, circulates it behind the firebox, and releases heated air back into the room to supplement the fire's radiant heat with convective heat.

ANDIRONS
Pairs of decorative metal stands that sit on the floor of the inner hearth to hold logs so that more oxygen can reach the underside of the burning wood.

ASH
Inorganic, mineral-laden powdery residue left after a wood fire.

ASHLAR
Blocks of stone, squared-up and fitted tightly together.

BAFFLES
Metal fins built into the interior of a stove to redirect and lengthen the path of the hot gases so that more heat is released into the room, and less out the chimney.

BEEHIVE OVEN
A brick oven with a domed top, designed particularly for baking.

BELLOWS
An implement of leather and wood used for pumping air into a wood-burning fire to introduce more oxygen.

BIOMASS FUELS
Natural or treated organic materials that burn steadily. Examples include traditional firewood and wood by-products formed into compressed pellets. Because they release carbon dioxide that is absorbed naturally by the planet's plant life, biomass fuels are considered an environmentally friendly alternative to fossil fuels.

BOX STOVE
A simple, one-chamber stove used for heating and stove-top cooking.

BRICK COURSING
A description of configuration, referring to the pattern of stacked bricks in a wall or chimney; three courses of brick typically measure 8 in. high.

BUILDING CODE
Legal statutes that outline regulations and standards for safe construction, installation, and use of building materials and appliances. Although national building codes apply, municipalities, counties, and states each employ a particular set of supplementary codes that citizens are obliged to follow.

BURN CHAMBER
The compartment inside a stove where the fire burns; also called a combustion chamber or firebox.

CARBON MONOXIDE
An odorless, tasteless poisonous gas emitted by a burning fire.

CATALYTIC COMBUSTOR
A multicelled, metal-coated ceramic disc placed inside a wood-burning stove to reduce the temperature at which a fire will burn to slow combustion, making wood fires last longer and burn more efficiently.

CERAMIC FLUE TILE
A square or rounded, hollow ceramic tile, stacked and mortared within a chimney to construct a continuous flue.

CHIMINEA
A small, outdoor heating stove with a bulb-shaped firebox. Traditionally made of fired clay and used to heat adobe homes in the Southwest and Mexico, chimineas are also manufactured today in cast iron or aluminum for outdoor use.

CHIMNEY
The vertical wood or brick passageway housing the flue used to vent a fire's smoke and fumes outdoors.

CHIMNEY CAP
A covering atop the termination of a chimney that shelters the chimney opening from precipitation, restricts flying sparks, and allows gaseous emissions to escape.

CHIMNEY SWEEP
A professional, often certified by the Chimney Safety Institute of America, trained to inspect, clean, and repair chimneys and fireplaces.

CHIMNEYBREAST
The wall of brick, cement, or stone above the fireplace opening that may project outward into the room.

CHIMNEYPIECE
The decorative assembly of wood, tile, metal, concrete, or stone surrounding the fireplace opening; today we call these mantelpieces.

CHIMNEY POT
A decorative extension of a chimney flue, usually of terra-cotta, to improve the fireplace's draft.

CHIMNEYSTACK
The entire assembly of fireplace and chimney.

CLADDING
A layer of finish material such as stone, tile, or wood applied to an exterior wall to preserve, beautify, or add decoration to the building.

CLINKER BRICKS
Bricks that are "manufacturer's seconds"—below standard due to an accidental shape or color but appealing for their whimsical charm.

COMBUSTION
The burning process in which a fuel such as wood, coal, or gas mixes with oxygen to produce the heat and light of fire.

COMBUSTION GASES
The chemical products of combustion, including carbon monoxide and carbon dioxide.

CORD OF WOOD
Cut, stacked pieces of firewood measuring 4 ft. by 4 ft. by 8 ft. or 128 cu. ft.

COVING
The vertical sides of the firebox, lined with heat-proof refractory brick, or firebrick. The covings are splayed, making a "V" that faces into a room, in order to radiate heat toward the fireplace opening and into the room.

CREOSOTE
A highly flammable by-product of fire combustion that can build up on a flue's inside walls.

CRICKET
A small portion of roof placed just behind a chimney to redirect rain and snow runoff so it won't pool between the chimney and the adjacent roof surface.

DAMPER
An adjustable metal panel, like a hinged door, that sits within the throat at the top of the firebox and can be manipulated to close off the fireplace or stove from the flue above when not in use.

DOWNDRAFT
Smoke or gas that is blown back down the flue from above and into the fireplace or stove.

DIRECT VENT
A gas-burning stove or fireplace that draws air for combustion directly from the outdoors and vents combustion by-products directly outside through a short, horizontal flue.

EFFICIENCY
A measurement based on the ratio between the amount of fuel used to create a heating fire and the amount of heat thus generated.

FENDER
A low barrier made of iron or brass that separates a firebox from the room to keep ashes and embers within the hearth area, away from flooring or rugs.

FIREBACK
A thick, cast iron plate installed at the rear interior wall of a fireplace to protect the back wall and help radiate the fire's heat into the room.

FIREBOX
The chamber within a stove or fireplace where the fire burns.

FIREBRICK
A type of brick manufactured and fired at a high temperature to ensure its capacity to withstand high heat.

FIREDOGS
A pair of cast iron stands that support the logs in a fireplace; also called andirons.

FIRE PIT
A manufactured vessel designed to burn either wood or gas in an outdoor setting; traditionally, a shallow hole dug in soil or sand for an outdoor bonfire or cooking fire.

FIRE SCREEN
A screen that is placed directly in front of the fireplace opening to block sparks and embers from entering the room.

FLUE
A pipe made of ceramic or metal through which combustion by-products move from the firebox, through the chimney, and doors.

FOSSIL FUEL
Inorganic, nonrenewable fuels, including coal, heating oil, propane, and natural gas.

FOUNDATION
The part of a building that sits below the ground to support and distribute the weight of the structure or fireplace above.

FRIEZE
The decorative vertical panel between the fireplace opening and a mantel shelf.

GOLDEN MEAN
A ratio of dimensions, based on the 1:1.618 proportion identified by the mathematician Pythagoras, which occurs in both the natural world and manmade forms and seems to be universally aesthetically pleasing.

GRATE
A basket-like, cast iron tray on legs upon which coal or wood are burned inside the firebox.

HEAD
The part of the surround that runs horizontally along the top of the fireplace opening, just beneath the frieze and above the firebox.

HEARTH
The fireplace's floor, often extending some distance into the room. Within the firebox, the inner hearth is faced with a heat-proof refractory material such as firebrick.

HEARTH EXTENSION
A floor area of noncombustible material such as stone or brick that extends outside the firebox into the room and provides a buffer zone for flying sparks or rolling embers.

HOOD
A metal or wooden awning, affixed to the face of the chimney-breast and flaring out over the top of the firebox into a room.

INGLENOOK
An architectural term for a cozy, built-in seating area near or surrounding a fireplace; also called a "chimney corner."

INSERT
A new stove installed within an existing masonry fireplace to improve the heat output and reduce drafts.

JAMB
One of the pair of the vertical portions of a mantelpiece framing the sides of a fireplace.

K-VALUE
The calculated measurement of a material's power to insulate; manufacturers must indicate a minimum K-value for the hearth on which their stove must safely sit.

KACHELOFEN
A freestanding, factory-made porcelain ceramic stove originating in northern Europe, often covered with colorful ceramic tiles.

KINDLING
Dry, slender sticks of wood, bundled newspaper, pinecones, or other easily ignitable material used to start a fire.

LINTEL
The horizontal structural member of metal or wood installed over a fireplace opening to support the structure above and distribute the weight to either side of the opening.

LISTED
Signifies that a manufactured stove or fireplace has been reviewed by Underwriter's Laboratory or other legitimate inspection agency to ensure its compliance with standards for safe use.

LOG SETS
Artificial logs made of refractory material that simulate actual logs for a gas fireplace.

MANTEL
Shortened form for the word mantelpiece, the ornamental structure surrounding a fireplace, framing the fireplace opening, and often providing a shelf above.

MANTEL SHELF
The horizontal portion of a decorative mantel that can be used for display.

MASONRY
The materials, art, and craft of stone, concrete, or brick construction.

MASONRY HEATER
A freestanding, site built woodburning brick or stone furnace with an internal masonry labyrinth to lengthen the path of the combustion gases so that more heat is extracted from the gases and stored in the masonry to radiate slowly over many hours.

MICA
Also known as isinglass, a mineral that can be sliced into thin, translucent sheets and withstand high temperatures; used for side panels in a parlor stove.

MORTAR
Bonding material, usually comprising lime and/or sand mixed with Portland cement, used in masonry to permanently attach stone, brick or tile.

NONVENTING
A type of gas- or gel-burning appliance that requires no venting to the outdoors. Combustion air is drawn from the room and combustion gases and by-products such as water vapor are exhausted back into the living space.

OVERMANTEL
A decorative arrangement of cabinetry, mirrors, and paneling installed above a mantel shelf.

PARLOR STOVE
A small, decorative, functional stove.

PARTICULATE EMISSIONS
Ash and soot residue from a fire emitted during combustion.

PELLET STOVE
A stove built to use pellets of fuel made of compressed sawdust or other biomass fuel.

PLATE STOVE
A colonial-era stove for cooking and heating whose firebox was constructed by a number of interlocking cast iron plates.

POKER
An iron rod used to adjust burning firewood for optimal combustion.

POTBELLIED STOVE
A wood- or coal-burning stove with a distinctive rounded profile, shaped like a pot belly.

PREFABRICATED FIREPLACE
A nonmasonry fireplace, factory manufactured for installation inside a home; see also Zero-clearance fireplace.

PYROLYSIS
The three-stage chemical reaction of fire in which heat transforms complex substances into simpler substances.

RADIANT HEAT
Heat transmitted by infrared radiation from a heat source, as opposed to heat transmitted by conduction (by direct exchange) or convection (through heated air).

REFRACTORY
Describes materials, such as bricks or cement, manufactured to withstand very high heat and thus suitable for use in fireplace, hearth, and chimney construction.

ROMAN BRICKS
Bricks manufactured in a longer-than-standard 12-in. lengths.

RUMFORD FIREPLACE
An elegantly tall, brick fireplace with a shallow firebox designed to radiate the maximum heat into a room designed by Benjamin Thompson, a.k.a. Count Rumford, a British loyalist in the mid-18th century American colonies.

SLIPS
A British term for the legs of a fireplace surround, i.e., the portions that run vertically along each side of the opening.

SMOKE CHAMBER
A bulbous area above the firebox, behind the throat, at the base of the flue.

SMOKE SHELF
The ledge at the bottom of the smoke chamber.

SOOT
A powdery black by-product of burning wood or coal, carried by smoke out of the firebox and up the flue.

SPARK ARRESTER
A metal screened cage installed atop a chimney flue to contain flying sparks.

STAINLESS STEEL FLUE LINER
A tubular insert designed for repair of a damaged ceramic flue

STEP STOVE
An antique type of stove with two compartments, one a firebox that heats the flat cooking surface above it and the other an oven that is heated by the same fire.

STOVE BLACKING
Powdered graphite, used on antique wood-burning stoves the way high-temperature paint is used today, to keep the stove from rusting.

STOVE BOARD
A flat hearth board made of noncombustible material that sits beneath an indoor stove to support the stove and protect the floor from heat and sparks.

STOVEPIPE
A segment of metal tubing, also known as chimney connector, that connects a stove's firebox to the flue of an existing nearby fireplace in the case of a retrofitted installation, or connects a new stove to a flue or chimney pipe.

SURROUND
The noncombustible brick, stone, metal, or tile border that frames the three sides of a fireplace opening.

TAPESTRY BRICK
Brick that is deliberately roughened during its manufacturing; traditionally popular in bungalow chimneys.

THIMBLE
An insulated sleeve for the flue to pass through at an opening in a wood partition, ceiling, or masonry chimneybreast, to protect surrounding materials from heat.

THROAT
The small opening at the top of a firebox top that leads to the flue. Most fireplaces include an adjustable metal damper to close the hroat when the fireplace is not in use.

UNDERWRITERS LABORATORIES (UL)
An independent organization that evaluates and certifies the safety compliance of light fixtures, appliances, and other consumer products, including factory-produced fireplaces and stoves.

VENTING
The process of exhausting smoke, fumes, and gases outdoors from a stove or fireplace either vertically or horizontally through a flue.

ZERO-CLEARANCE FIREPLACE
A factory-built fireplace that is constructed and insulated so that it can be placed safely in close proximity to combustible materials such as wood framing.

Resources

TRADE AND CONSUMER ORGANIZATIONS, FAQ SITES, AND GOVERNMENT WEBSITES

California Energy Commission
www.consumerenergycenter.org/homeandwork/homes/inside/heatandcool/fireplaces.html
Offers consumer tips on selecting products

Central Pot Spotting Authority of Great Britain and Ireland (CPSA)
www.users.breathe.com/yorick/potspot/
"Official" site of the pot spotting organization with history and handbook

Chimney Safety Institute of America
www.csia.org
Nonprofit, educational organization dedicated to chimney and venting system safety

Environmental Protection Agency
www.epa.gov/woodstoves/index.html
Consumer information and list of certified stove models and manufacturers

Fireplace Lowdown
www.sicarius.typepad.com/fireplace_lowdown/
Articles and tips about fireplaces and stoves

Fireplaces
www.fireplaces.com
Tips and advice for homeowners who are seeking to install a new fireplace or upgrade an existing one

Fireplaces and Wood Stoves
www.fireplacesandwoodstoves.com
Online consumer guide for fireplaces, wood stoves, and accessories

Green Trust Sustainability & Renewable Energy
www.green-trust.org
Educational information on biofuels and methods of living cleanly and efficiently

Hearth, Patio, and Barbecue Association
www.hpba.org
Trade association representing and promoting the interests of the hearth products industry in North America; holds an annual exposition

HearthNet
www.hearth.com
Consumer information on hearth products, hundreds of articles, and classifieds

Masonry Heater Association of North America
www.mha-net.org
An association that shapes regulations, standards, and codes, and informs and educates the public

Masonry Institute of America
www.masonryinstitute.org
A promotional, technical, and research organization established to improve and extend the use of masonry

The National Fire Protection Association
www.nfpa.org
The world's leading advocate of fire prevention, providing codes and standards to reduce fire and other hazards to the quality of life

National Fireplace Institute
www.nficertified.org
Establishes credentials for professionals involved in planning and installing residential hearth appliances and venting systems.

Pellet Fuels Institute
www.pelletheat.org
Nonprofit association that educates consumers about the convenience and practicality of using wood pellet fuel in both residential and commercial applications

The Russian Stove
www.russianstove.com
Information on constructing a masonry heater, or Russian stove

Underwriters Laboratory
www.ul.com
Consumer product safety standards and certification.

U.S. Department of Energy
www.eere.energy.gov/consumer/
Consumer guide to energy efficiency and renewable energy

Wood Energy Technology Transfer, Inc.
www.wettinc.ca.
Nonprofit training and education association that promotes the safe and effective use of wood burning systems in Canada

The Wood Heat Organization
www.woodheat.org
Nonprofit, nongovernmental agency dedicated to the responsible use of wood as a home heating fuel

CONTRIBUTING MANUFACTURERS AND FABRICATORS

American Energy Systems Inc.
www.magnumheat.com
Corn-burning stoves

American Gas Log Company Inc.
888-484-7293
Gas fireplace log sets

Antique Stoves
www.antiquestoves.com
Antique stoves, parts, appraisals, restorations, and accessories

Buckley Rumford Company
www.rumford.com
Custom designed and crafted Rumford fireplaces, articles, and consultations

Burley Appliances Ltd.
www.burleyappliances.com
Electric fireplaces

CFM Products
www.vermontcastings.com
Gas-burning, wood-burning, and electric fireplaces, inserts and stoves, mantels, and accessories

Chimney Pot Shoppe
www.chimneypot.com
Ceramic chimney pots

Condar Company
www.condar.com
Fireplaces, catalytic combustors, gel flames, and accessories

Dell-Point Pellet Stoves
www.pelletstove.com
Pellet stoves

Fire Rock Manufacturing Inc.
www.firerock.us
Prefabricated lightweight concrete fireplace components

Fireorb/Cool Warmth Company
www.fireorb.net
Spun-steel fireplaces

Heat & Glo
www.heatnglo.com
Gas-burning, wood-burning, and electric fireplaces, inserts and stoves, mantels, and accessories

Lennox Hearth Products
www.lennoxhearthproducts.com
Gas-burning, wood-burning, pellet and electric fireplaces, inserts and stoves, and accessories

Moberg Fireplaces
www.mobergfireplaces.com
Custom-designed and crafted fireplaces and fireplace components

Solus Decor Inc.
www.solusdecor.com
Prefabricated lightweight concrete mantelpieces

Sud-Chemie Prototech Inc.
www.sud-chemie.com
Catalytic combustors

Trikeenan Tileworks, Inc.
www.trikeenan.com
Decorative ceramic tile

Index

Index note: page references in italics indicate a photograph; page references in bold indicate an illustration.

Credits

p. ii: © JK Lawrence/ www.jklawrencephoto.com, Design: Custom Log Homes, Stevensville, MT, www.customlog.com

p. iii: © Tim Street-Porter

p. vi: © Brian Vanden Brink (top), © Rob Karosis (middle), ©Carolyn Bates (bottom)

p. 1: © JK Lawrence (top), © Burley (middle), © Jessie Walker (bottom)

p. 2: © Brian Vanden Brink

p. 3: © Tim Street-Porter

Chapter 1

pp. 4–5: © Rob Karosis

p. 6: © Scot Zimmerman

p. 7: © Mark Samu

p. 8: © Carolyn Bates

p. 9: © Brian Vanden Brink (top), © Charles Miller (bottom)

p. 10: © Tim Street-Porter

p. 11: © Brian Vanden Brink

p. 12: © Jessie Walker

p. 13: © R.L. Johnson, Atlantic Archives

p. 14: © Brian Vanden Brink

p. 15: © Brian Vanden Brink (top), photo courtesy Fire Orb (bottom)

p. 16: © Robert Benson (top), © Mark Samu (bottom)

p. 17: © Carolyn Bates

p. 18: © JK Lawrence/ www.jklawrencephoto.com, Design: Architect: Richard Dooley, 2996 Grandview Drive, Atlanta, GA

p. 19: © Charles Bickford (top), © Eric Roth (bottom)

p. 20: © Carolyn Bates (top), © Rob Karosis (bottom)

p. 21: © Eric Roth (top), © Mark Samu (bottom)

p. 22: © Roger Turk (top), © Carolyn Bates (bottom)

p. 23: © Brian Vanden Brink (top), © Roger Turk (bottom)

Chapter 2

p. 24: © Brian Vanden Brink

p. 25: © Eric Roth

p. 26: © Charles Bickford

p. 27: © Brian Vanden Brink

p. 28: © Rob Karosis

p. 29: © Mark Samu

p. 30: © Jeff Heatley, Stelle Architects (top), © Mark Samu (bottom)

p. 31: © Tim Street-Porter

p. 32: © Carolyn Bates

p. 33: © Brian Vanden Brink

p. 35: © Scot Zimmerman

p. 36: photo courtesy FireRock (top), © Carolyn Bates (bottom)

p. 37: photo courtesy Moberg Fireplaces

p. 38: © Charles Miller

p. 39: © Carolyn Bates (top left), © Tim Street-Porter (bottom left)

p. 40: © Carolyn Bates (top left), © Brian Vanden Brink (top right), Jessie Walker (bottom right)

p. 41: © Carolyn Bates

p. 42: © Brian Vanden Brink

p. 43: © Tim Street-Porter (top), © Brian Vanden Brink (bottom)

p. 44: © Rob Karosis

p. 45: © Robert Benson (top), © Brian Vanden Brink (bottom)

p. 46: © Rob Karosis

p. 47: © Brian Vanden Brink

p. 48: © Tim Street-Porter (left), © Chris Adams (top & bottom right)

p. 49: © Robert Benson

p. 50: © Brian Vanden Brink

p. 51: © Carolyn Bates (top), © Sandy Agrofiotis (bottom)

p. 52: © Carolyn Bates

p. 53: © Brian Vanden Brink (top) © Lisa Romerein (bottom)

p. 54: © J. K. Lawrence

p. 55: © J. K. Lawrence/ www.jklawrencephoto.com Design: Click's Construction, Belgrade, MT, www.clicksconstruction.com

p. 56: © Brian Vanden Brink

p. 57: © Carolyn Bates (top), © Brian Vanden Brink (bottom)

p. 58: © Mark Samu

pp. 59–61: © Brian Vanden Brink

p. 62: © Tim Street-Porter

p. 63: © Brian Vanden Brink

p. 64: © Carolyn Bates

p. 65: photo courtesy The Chimneypot Shoppe

p. 66: © Roger Turk (top), © Carolyn Bates (bottom)

p. 67: © Brian Vanden Brink

p. 68: © Anton Grassl

p. 69: © Tim Street-Porter

p. 70: © Carolyn Bates

p. 71: © Charles Miller

p. 72: © Fred Housel

p. 73: © Robert Benson

Chapter 3

p. 74: © Richard Vitullo

p. 75: © Jessie Walker

p. 76: © Eric Roth (right), © Jessie Walker (bottom)

p. 77: © Sandy Agrafiotis

p. 78: © Brian Vanden Brink (top), © Carolyn Bates (bottom)

p. 79: © Jessie Walker

p. 80: © Rob Karosis

p. 81: © Brian Vanden Brink (top), © Bruce Buck (bottom)

p. 82: © Brian Vanden Brink

p. 83: © Rob Karosis

p. 84: © Brian Vanden Brink

p. 85: © Tim Street-Porter (top), © Eric Roth (bottom)

p. 86: © Tim Street-Porter (top), © Carolyn Bates (bottom)

p. 87: © Brackett

p. 88: © Carolyn Bates

p. 89: © Richard Leo Johnson (left), © Rob Karosis (bottom)

p. 90: © Rob Karosis

p. 91: © Eric Roth

pp. 92–93: © Brian Vanden Brink

p. 94: © Eric Roth (right)

© Robert Perron (bottom)

p. 95: © J K Lawrence/ www.jklawrencephoto.com Design: Kelly Davis, AIA/Sala Architects, Inc., Stillwater, MN, www.salarc.com (top), © Lisa Romerein (bottom)

p. 96: Carolyn Bates (top), Rob Karosis (bottom)

p. 97: © Scot Zimmerman

p. 98: © Brian Vanden Brink (top), © Lisa Romerein (bottom)

p. 99: © Jessie Walker

p. 100: © Rob Karosis

p. 101: photo courtesy Solus (left), © James Yochum (bottom)

p. 102: © Tim Street-Porter

p. 103: photo courtesy Trikeenan Tile

p. 104 © Mark Samu

p. 105: © Brian Vanden Brink

p. 106: © Robert Benson

p. 107: © Robert Benson (top left), © Roger Turk (top right), © Eric Roth (bottom left), © Brian Vanden Brink (bottom right)

p. 108: © Steve Vierra

p. 109: © Jessie Walker (top),

© Bruce Buck (bottom left),

© Eric Roth (bottom right)

p. 110: © Carolyn Bates

p. 111: © Scot Zimmerman (top), © Charles Bickford (bottom)

p. 112: © Eric Roth

p. 113: © Carolyn Bates

Chapter 4

pp. 114–116: © Brian Vanden Brink

p. 117: © Mark Samu

p. 118: © J. K. Lawrence / www.jklawrencephoto.com

Design: Jack Jackson, AIA/Eastbound Design Group, Eastbound, WA, 360-376-4057

p. 119: © Carolyn Bates

p. 120: © Brian Vanden Brink (top), © J. K. Lawrence / www.jklawrencephoto.com, Design: Greene Partners Architecture & Design, Lopez, WA/www.greenepartners .com (bottom right), © Eric Roth (bottom left)

p. 121: © J. K. Lawrence (top), photo courtesy Sud Chemie (bottom)

p. 122: © Rob Karosis (top)

p. 123: photo courtesy Vermont Castings

p. 124–125: © Brian Vanden Brink

p. 126: © Michael Grimm, Stelle Architects (top), © Jessie Walker (bottom)

p. 127: © Carolyn Bates

p, 128: © J.K. Lawrence / www.jklawrencephoto.comDesign: Richard Fernau, AIA/Furnau & Hartman Architects, Berkeley, CA, 510-848-7010

p. 129: photo courtesy Vermont Castings (top), © Brian Vanden Brink (bottom)

p. 130: © Brian Vanden Brink

p. 131: © Rob Karosis

p. 132: © Eric Roth

p. 133: © Jessie Walker (bottom), photo courtesy Mercer Museum (top)

p. 134: © Edward Semmelroth (top), © Jessie Walker (bottom)

p. 135: © Carolyn Bates (top), © Brian Vanden Brink (bottom)

p. 136: © Eric Roth

p. 137: © J. K. Lawrence/ www.jklawrencephoto.comDesign: Tulikivi by WarmStone Fireplaces & Designs, Livingston, MT, www.warmstone.com

p. 138: © J. K. Lawrence

p. 139: © Jessie Walker (top), © Carolyn Bates (bottom)

p. 140: © Robert Perron (left), photo courtesy Vermont Castings (right)

p. 141: © Carolyn Bates (top), © Jessie Walker (bottom)

Chapter 5

p. 142: © Carolyn Bates

p. 143: © Roger Turk

p. 144: © Steve Vierra

p. 145: © Brian Vanden Brink

p. 146: © Roger Turk (top), © Scot Zimmerman (bottom)

p. 147: photo courtesy Heat & Glo (top), © J K Lawrence/ www.jklawrencephoto.com Design: Place Architecture, Bozeman, MT, www.placearch.com (bottom)

p. 148: © Jessie Walker

p. 149: © Jessie Walker (top), © J. K. Lawrence / www.jklawrencephoto.com Design: Graham Goff/Goff Architecture, Bozeman, MT and Hendricks Fine Homes, Bozeman, MT (bottom)

p. 150: © Roger Turk

p. 151: © Tim Street-Porter

p. 152: © Roger Turk (top), © Scot Zimmerman (right)

p. 153: photo courtesy Heat & Glo

p. 154: photo courtesy Solus

p. 155: photo courtesy Lennox Hearth Products (left), photo courtesy Alladin (right)

pp. 156–157: photos courtesy Dell-Point Pellet Stove

p. 158: Burley (top), © Carolyn Bates (right)

p. 159: © Scot Zimmerman

p. 160: © Scot Zimmerman

p. 161: photo courtesy Condar (top), © Rob Karosis (bottom)

Chapter 6

p. 162: © Mark Samu

p. 163: © Scot Zimmerman

p. 164: © Roger Turk (right), © Scot Zimmerman (left), © Carolyn Bates (bottom)

p. 165: © Jessie Walker

p. 166–167: Brian Vanden Brink

p. 168: © Brian Vanden Brink (left), © Chipper Hatter (right)

p. 169: © Scot Zimmerman

p. 170: © Ross Chapin

p. 171: © Chipper Hatter (top), photo courtesy Heat & Glo (bottom)

p. 172: © Scot Zimmerman

p. 173: © Eric Roth (top), © Rob Karosis (bottom)

p. 174: photo courtesy Condar

p. 175: © Scot Zimmerman

p. 176: © Jessie Walker (right), © Lisa Romerein (left)

p. 177: © Mark Samu (top) © Chipper Hatter (bottom)

p. 178: © Jessie Walker (top), © Lisa Romerein (bottom)

p. 179: © Carolyn Bates

p. 180: © Scot Zimmerman

p. 181: © Scot Zimmerman (left) © Eric Roth (right)

p. 182: © Deirdre Walpole

p. 183: © Lisa Romerein

pp. 184–185: © J. K. Lawrence/ www.jklawrencephoto.com Design: Alpine Log Homes, Victor, MT, www.alpineloghomes.com

p. 186: © Brian Vanden Brink

p. 187: © Carolyn Bates (left), © Scot Zimmerman (right)